WESTMAR COLLEGE

W9-BQY-993

WESTMAR COLLEGE LIBRARY

ENGLISH
CONGREGATIONAL
HYMNS IN THE
EIGHTEENTH
CENTURY

ENGLISH CONGREGATIONAL HYMNS IN THE EIGHTEENTH CENTURY

Madeleine Forell Marshall
and Janet Todd

104894

THE UNIVERSITY PRESS OF KENTUCKY

Copyright © 1982 by The University Press of Kentucky

Scholarly publisher for the Commonwealth,
serving Berea College, Centre College of Kentucky,
Eastern Kentucky University, The Filson Club,
Georgetown College, Kentucky Historical Society,
Kentucky State University, Morehead State University,
Murray State University, Northern Kentucky University,
Transylvania University, University of Kentucky,
University of Louisville, and Western Kentucky University.

Editorial and Sales Offices: Lexington, Kentucky 40506-0024

Library of Congress Cataloging in Publication Data

Marshall, Madeleine Forell, 1946–
  English congregational hymns in the eighteenth century.

  Includes bibliographical references and index.
  1. Hymns, English—History and criticism. I. Todd,
Janet M., 1942–   II. Title.
BV312.M28   1982   264′.2   82-40176
ISBN 0-8131-1470-5

Contents

❦ I ❧

The Congregational Hymn:
Requirements & Resources

The Challenge of Hymnology

The congregational hymn as it came into being in the eighteenth century is a highly distinctive type of religious poetry, easily recognized by the metrical limits within which the hymn writer labored and by the short lines and stanzaic repetition required of congregational song. Despite such instant formal recognizability of hymns as hymns, the scholar who attempts a simple definition of the genre in terms of either its purpose or its content encounters immediate difficulty, the result of the varied uses to which hymns were put and the many different subjects and spiritual states that hymns were designed to treat. To say, for example, that a hymn is "sung praise" is as inaccurate as calling a sonnet the expression of love for a woman. Too many important items in the tradition become exceptions to the definition. In this instance, hymns telling Bible stories or expressing spiritual anxiety are most obviously excluded. Moreover, while the hymns are arranged metrically to allow singing, it is needlessly restrictive to insist that they are only hymns when they are sung. Hymns were read in private as well as sung in public and, like the psalms on which they were modeled, were available for many purposes.

The predominant characteristic of hymns, however expressive of conviction or religious passion they may be, may only be described as their impersonality. Religious verse that proceeds spontaneously, from the soul, as the private expression of the individual, is wholly inappropriate for congregational use. Even if the experience of the poet is commonplace and his expression is of general usefulness to other Christians, the resulting poem is not suitable for hymn use unless it is doctrinally correct and spiritually edifying. A congregation

of worshipers may be asked to sing only an expression of proper and
devout religious feeling. The irregular, highly original, or otherwise
extraordinary perception is unacceptable. In a given hymn, if a hymn
writer is indeed expressing religious feeling, it must be communal
rather than private. The convictions found in the hymns of the past
thus provide an index to the acceptable, approved, and recommended
doctrine and spiritual response at a particular time within a given
Protestant tradition, yielding a great quantity of information about
popular religious feeling that is inaccessible elsewhere.

While congregational requirements effectively distinguish hymns
from private religious lyrics, the hymns certainly remain poetry,
which takes the expression of private or collective feeling as only one
of its purposes. It is not accidental that the rise of the English hymn
coincides with the great era of didactic literature in England and that
Isaac Watts, the clergyman who wrote the first hymns that we may
regard as belonging to the continuous English tradition, was es-
teemed as an educator. Accordingly, many hymns are the artful
expressions of religious truth, designed to be learned in song as
musical recitation. While recitation may be unfamiliar in our era of
textbook and audiovisual education, its efficacy was unquestioned by
our ancestors.

Expressive and didactic aims are linked in those hymns that are
meant to teach righteous sentiment, rehearsing the singers in the true
Christian response to a joyful event, disappointment, despair, temptation, the Nativity, or the Crucifixion. The singers' possibly errant
feelings are corrected in the fashion of contemporary exemplary
literature as the hymn writer skillfully exploits the situation in which
the singers recite his words, making them their own. This collective
recitation of the verse of a modern poet, unhallowed by biblical
authority, was a startling development in the English tradition.
Church of England reservations about admitting hymns to the service
are understandable.

The hymns may be usefully viewed, from a third perspective, as
religious entertainment, in which the dramatic potential of biblical
material is enthusiastically developed. Vivid tableaux display scenes
from the Old and New Testaments. The quantity of direct discourse
in many storytelling hymns and its tone often recalls contemporary
heroic and domestic drama. Such hymns become participatory religious theater, the many injunctions to "see," "look," and "behold"

suggesting a dramatic self-consciousness on the part of both writers and singers, an awareness that they are involved in a large-scale religious production. The musical theatricality of many of these hymns reminds the reader of the contemporary flowering of the opera and of the fact that J. F. Lampe, a Covent Garden musician, contributed many hymn tunes.

It is by viewing the hymns in such a context of eighteenth-century literature and literary purpose that we may come to an accurate description of their nature as poetry and their place in literary tradition. The study of hymns also promises to yield a rich harvest to the student of secular literature. Since these poems were presumably not dictated by God to their devout authors, they are unavoidably expressions of the literary education and orientation of the time. Minor poetry, as hymns may be, is frequently an excellent index to the taste of a given period as well as to a generally accepted world view of an age. In the hymns of Watts, written in the early part of the century, for example, the peaceful coexistence of "metaphysical" wit and Augustan values indicates a catholicity of taste that defies modern categorization and refines the literary historian's appreciation of the interpenetration of literary periods. The place and nature of the cult of sensibility in the Wesleyan revival is revealed in Charles Wesley's hymns. John Newton and William Cowper demonstrate the adaptation of the hymn to the changing view of both poetry and the human situation that characterized the second half of the eighteenth century.

Finally, hymn research promises an improved understanding of the religion of the eighteenth century. It may be suggested that the variety and complexity of religious experience of the era have been sadly underestimated. Literary historians have tended to regard religious convictions they do not share as insignificant, to reduce vital matters of belief to mere labels (deist, Anglican, Methodist), and often to dismiss the issue as immaterial. At the other extreme, partisan historians have eulogized their denominational heroes, at the expense of any profitable objectivity. In these pages we seek to treat the hymns as literature and theology as a significant human concern, both of which are accessible to the student.

Hymnology is a venerable endeavor that has been pursued through the years with great love and dedication by numerous worthy scholars. The nature and scope of three classic works of criticism suggest both the specialized resources available to the hymnologist and the complexity of our double task of definition and historical placement.

In 1892 John Julian published his *Dictionary of Hymnology,* giving the sources and history of almost all hymns in English.[1] It is still a key reference work, and its contents demonstrate the rich and varied heritage of hymns, which may have been taken from the Old or New Testaments verbatim, may have been loosely paraphrased, or may have been intentionally or unintentionally laced with biblical language and allusions. Hymns may be translations of traditional or modern material, wholly original compositions, or any combination of the two. Moreover, the utilitarian aspect of hymns has created and continues to create considerable textual difficulty. Frequently hymns are substantially changed, cut, or expanded or their language is altered to suit the requirements of a given collection. Such procedure is acceptable, analogous to the freedom that a director enjoys in shaping the text of a play. Hymns, like drama, are living texts. The rarity of carefully worked editions showing variations and derivations remains a major obstacle to authoritative hymn study.

Louis Benson's monumental work *The English Hymn: Its Development and Use in Worship* appeared in 1915.[2] It remains the authoritative history, to which every student of the hymn is unavoidably indebted. Benson traced the extensive heritage of the hymn, explaining its relations to antecedent liturgical and extraliturgical religious verse in various Protestant and Catholic traditions. The limitations of the book are an inevitable product of its age. New perspectives on baroque, neoclassical, and romantic literature have rendered much of the literary historical material obsolete.

In his opening pages, Benson reveals a second problem, one of approach, that has frequently undermined the hymnologists' attempts to progress beyond cataloging and the textual study of hymns. Benson wrote:

The truth is that if the methods of the literary historian are not misapplied to Hymnody, they are at least inadequate. A hymn may or may not happen to be literature; in any case it is something more. Its sphere, its motive, its canons and its use are different. It belongs with the things of the spirit, in the sphere of religious experience and communion with God. Its special sphere is worship, and its fundamental relations are not literary but liturgical. [P. viii]

Benson wanted hymns to be examined only devoutly, but this desire led him to underrate their literary potential, for "literature" is a term broad in scope, embracing kinds as disparate in quality and purpose as *Paradise Lost* and the poetry of Herbert, *The Rape of the Lock* and *Gulliver's Travels*. We have suggested that why poets write hymns, what principles they follow and within what limits they work, the literary taste of poet and singer alike, the relationship of hymns to other literature, and similar critical questions are legitimate and their answers useful. However profound the religious experience conveyed by the hymn, however inspired the form by its spiritual content, the diction, figurative language, and verbal design of the hymns are human creations dependent on the literary tradition within which the poet is working. (A modern inversion of Benson's hesitation would seem to underestimate not literary history but religion. The general modern neglect of hymns by scholars primarily interested in literary history reflects a prejudice against religious subject matter and inevitably results in partial history.)

The third essential reference work on the hymnologist's shelf, indicating a third important feature of the study of hymns, is Erik Routley's *The Music of Christian Hymnody*. The bond between hymn text and tune is very strong, and familiar hymns can be considered apart from the traditional tunes only with the greatest difficulty. Routley describes the new music written in England after the Restoration and the collections of new psalm tunes that appeared at the beginning of the eighteenth century, providing new possibilities for metrical variation. In 1742 the *Foundery Collection* of forty tunes, designed as a supplement to other music books, showed the influence of Handel on hymn music. In 1745 John Wesley met J. F. Lampe, a bassoon player at Covent Garden, and a year later the converted Lampe edited the music of *Hymns for the Greater Festivals,* which demonstrated the "operatic-aria technique[s], which are so characteristic of Methodist tunes."[3] The music to which a hymn is sung must match the tone and taste of the lyrics. The musical development traced by Routley was both the cause and the result of the rise and proliferation of hymn texts.

Further and more recent scholarship has treated the language and rhetorical tools, biblical sources, and the structure of many hymns. Carefully worked critical editions of some hymns are available. Scholars have traced the influence of particular hymns on Blake and Emily

Dickinson. It is a great misfortune that most such effort has been seriously marred by a number of failures peculiar to hymnologists. We shall review these failures only because they may warn us of the pitfalls of hymn study.

The first problem is the most common and perhaps the least dangerous except as it jeopardizes the status of hymnology as a scholarly and objective discipline. Intensely partisan criticism, verging on adulation, seems to attach itself particularly to the hymns of Charles Wesley. Loyalty to a Protestant tradition often seems to inspire hymnological undertakings and to undermine their avowed critical purpose. With little explanation Bernard Lord Manning claimed that the *Hymns for People Called Methodists*

ranks in Christian literature with the Psalms, the Book of Common Prayer, the Canon of the Mass. In its own way, it is perfect, unapproachable, elemental in its perfection. You cannot alter it except to mar it; it is a work of supreme devotional art by a religious genius. You may compare it with Leonardo's 'Last Supper' or King's Chapel; and, as Blackstone said of the English Constitution, the proper attitude to take to it is this: we must venerate where we are not able presently to comprehend.[4]

While such fervor may be admirable in a churchman, it is reprehensible in a critic of literature, minor or great.

Equally unilluminating is the rhapsodical acclamation of Wesley indulged in by Ernest Rattenbury: "Charles did not dissect, analyse, and weigh truth; he did not relate it to this or that philosophical system; he was not a theological botanist. His hymns are not museum pieces; they are flowers in a flower garden; his doctrines are alive."[5] If hymns are flowers they are indeed beyond the reach of literary scholarship. It is more useful, however, to see them as rationally wrought works of art, designed for a purpose within a tradition of hymn writing and singing. While Rattenbury sometimes made acute observations about the literary characteristics of hymns, his critical focus generally failed when he attempted to draw useful conclusions. Even Martha England, whose work on hymns shows the most "literary" reading of the texts, declares with little explanation that Blake cannot stand comparison with Wesley as a religious poet.[6]

This critical failure is especially obvious to one accustomed to a more objective scholarship (whether or not the objectivity is genuine). Perhaps less obvious, at least to those unfamiliar with the humanistic wealth and diversity of the eighteenth century, is the extent to which scholars who have written about hymns of the age have bound themselves to views of the period that are no longer tenable. The eighteenth century is generally assumed to have been one of the most depraved ages of English history, saved from destruction only by the evangelical revival.[7] For Hoxie Neale Fairchild, for example, faith seems to have been practically the invention of the Methodists, leaving Dean Swift certainly among the many unredeemed: "Scores of Swift's poems could hardly have been written by a man of religious nature, while none of them reveals the slightest trace of a reverent and loving personal faith in any sort of Divine Power."[8] Proponents of this view of Augustan faith and morality proceed with blinders on. Such an approach will necessarily undermine any attempt to see hymns as integral to the age in which their authors lived.

A yet more subtle threat to the careful placement of hymns in relation to other literature of the eighteenth century is the general prejudice of hymnologists against eighteenth-century poetry. Many hymn scholars identify any expression of feeling in verse or any use of common vocabulary as an indication of the coming of romanticism. Robert Tudur Jones wrote of Watts: "his greatest hymns pulsate with an emotion which is prophetic of the emphasis on feeling and personal experience which was such a close link between Methodist hymnody and the Romantic Movement in literature."[9] This connection between hymns and romanticism is as difficult to justify as it is frequently presumed. We suggested above that in its quality and purpose the emotion expressed in hymns intended for congregational use is depersonalized and doctrinally corrected, thereby differing from the more individual emotion shown by lyrics. Second, it is not clear how a connection between hymns and romanticism could be established, since historical relations are causal and influential. The antecedents of hymns are best examined for clues to the presence of emotion in poetry when it may be unexpected. Third, the Augustan era is unjustly accused of lacking "emphasis on feeling and personal experience." The literature of sentiment, the *Journal to Stella*, and a goodly quantity of fine poetry refute any such claim. We do better to avoid such prophecy.

Mark Noll, as recently as 1974, perpetuated the narrow view of eighteenth-century literature, which ignores Steele, much of Pope and Swift, and certainly Richardson: "Charles Wesley, with the Romantics, rejected the artificiality, the aloofness, the autocracy of diction which

dominated eighteenth century English poetry; in so doing, both
Wesley and the Romantics freed themselves to deal with new
subjects and emotions which had been banned under the iron rule of
neoclassicism."[10] There was no iron rule of neoclassicism in
England. In their haste to approve of hymns as literature, the
hymnologists have rushed to label them preromantic, an act that has
created more problems by far than it has solved if our effort is to
determine what hymns are and how they suit the literary tradition of
which they are unavoidably a part.

Faulty history results in faulty reading of hymns, which leads in
turn to a misunderstanding of the nature and purpose of hymns.
Error's train is admirably illustrated by Noll's use of Charles Wesley's
rallying hymn "Come, O my guilty Brethren, come" as evidence of
Wesley's romantic inclinations:

> Come, O my guilty Brethren, come,
>   Groaning beneath your load of sin!
> His bleeding heart shall make you room,
>   His open side shall take you in.
> He calls you now, invites you home—
> Come, O my guilty Brethren, come! [P. 200]

In discerning an indulgence in feeling and a love for common humanity, which may or may not be romantic, this critic misses the obvious
fact that exhortation to communal entry into the pleura is quite alien
to the romantic world view.

The romantic association is perhaps to blame for the most serious
misunderstanding of the hymns as literature, graver even than any
confusion of hymns with religious lyrics. Because hymns are widely
known, they have been compared to popular, even folk, literature.
Noll wrote: "balladry and Wesley's hymns have great similarity:
poems for popular consumption, simple and direct, freed from the
neoclassical artificiality of diction, and—in many instances—rising
through clarity of thought, dramatic movement, and powerful emotion to the status of consequential poetry" (p. 201). Leaving aside
musical features, including stanzaic arrangement, metrical considera-
tions, and singability, such a comparison of ballads with hymns,
particularly the hymns of Wesley, is totally unsuitable. The anony-
mous composition, secular content, and narrative purpose of ballads
all distinguish them from hymns, which are of known authorship,

officially approved for Christian use and, to a greater or lesser extent, didactic in purpose. These features and the purported simplicity and directness of hymns will be treated with reference to particular hymn texts in the following chapters.

In his 1976 Clark lectures, "Literature of Dissent," Donald Davie went even further, describing the lyrical-tribal qualities of hymns, characterizing them as orally transmitted literature of the people rather than as poetry of the literary elite.[11] While such a political direction of study might be open to the hymnologist interested primarily in the popular love of hymns and their frequent oral transmission, it is certainly not relevant to the study of eighteenth-century hymns, which were book-bound literature composed by a literary elite and published under the watchful eyes of sectarian leaders. On the other hand, the popularity of hymns is certainly one motive for the literary study of them. Millions of Christians have committed dozens of hymns to memory, unaware that they know hundreds of lines of poetry by heart. Hymns are doubtless the most widely familiar poetic genre, and it may be that this familiarity profoundly influences other aspects of popular literary taste. Such investigation is, however, contingent on the careful definition and placement of hymns. Meanwhile, tribal-lyrical suggestions regarding hymns are only confusing; they ignore the hymn as an artful composition by literary men in the eighteenth century.

Accordingly, in this study we shall trace the development of the dissenting and evangelical hymn in the eighteenth century as it is seen in four major representative writers, with a view toward clarifying the characteristics of the genre along the lines suggested above. We anticipate that particular attention to the hymn genre and its historical development, in response to the special requirements imposed on the form, will facilitate the proper assignment of hymns to their due place in the history of English literature. If the effort at definition and placement succeeds, it should provide a base for more sophisticated investigation of the texts and language of the hymns, the relation of hymn verse and music, and the complex nature of religious experience of the period.

For our purposes there is certain danger in inclusiveness. Conscientious examination of all English hymns written to be sung would obscure, as it has in the past, the clear patterns in the development of the genre. Furthermore, zealous study of only the 9,000 hymns of

Charles Wesley significantly dulls the critical sensibility. Instead we have chosen hymn writers of the century who represented the major dissenting and evangelical traditions, the groups who sang hymns. Watts stands for Calvinist Independency in both his verse and his prose. Charles Wesley is a central figure in the Methodist revival. John Newton adhered to what may be called Calvinist evangelicalism within the Anglican church. The hymns of William Cowper, fourth and last, enable us to relate our conclusions about hymns to standard literary history. The four authors provide a sampling of the religious tastes and opinions characteristic of those groups who sang hymns. The hymns they wrote are accordingly distinct.[12]

Isaac Watts (1674–1748) was a leading Independent preacher and educator, whose prose and piety won him the admiration of Dr. Johnson. He wrote treatises on the religious discipline of the passions, the practice of prayer, and the right use of logic. He wrote as well some 200 hymns, which are characterized by the highly dramatic presentation of religious material and immediate, even grotesque imagery. As Watts's hymns were among the earliest designed for congregational singing, they demonstrate the relationship between metrical psalms and hymns and help us understand the controversy surrounding the revolutionary departure from English tradition. The tension reflected in both the language and content of Watts's hymns, between, on the one hand, conventional eighteenth-century values and poetic taste and, on the other, a rather violent conviction of human depravity and the appeal of asceticism, necessarily encourages us to reconsider the religious and poetic options of the times.

With Charles Wesley (1707–1788) we turn to the Methodist revival, which remained within the Anglican church throughout our period. As hymns were not sung in Anglican churches, Wesley's hymns were written for meetings and devotions rather than for liturgical services, a difference in purpose that tells in the design. The Calvinist theology of Watts's hymns is, of course, absent from those of Wesley, which preach the universal availability of salvation. The Wesleyan hymns follow in theory the practice of Watts and the accepted use of the metrical psalms, but the religious focus has become almost totally individual. Watts wanted to teach his people to voice familiar devotional states, while Wesley taught his people to feel religiously. Extreme emotional response was expected of the believer. The grotesque tableaux of the Crucifixion familiar in Watts's hymns were subordinated to the reactions of the singers. As we have suggested, the relationship that this lesson in subjectivity bears to contemporary literature is complex. Certainly religious *experience* has always been subjective, and we cannot automatically link Wesleyan excesses to either the cult of sensibility or romanticism. The prominent place accorded general education by the Methodists becomes relevant, and Wesley's hymns are usefully approached as didactic-sentimental literature. Just as the exemplary Pamela taught her readers how they should cope with moral dilemmas, so the persona of Charles Wesley's hymns demonstrated correct devotional response. If Wesley's hymns are not precisely sentimental, at any rate they show the adaptation of the methods of the literature of sensibility to the ends of evangelical education.

John Newton (1725–1807), like Charles Wesley an ordained Anglican minister, was a noted Calvinist evangelical leader and propagandist. His hymns were written for the education, comfort, and entertainment of the particular congregation at Olney. This specificity and Newton's image of himself as priest distinguish his hymns from the work of his predecessors. His best hymns contain direct, powerful images, laden with significance derived either from Newton's own life story or from the suitability of the Gospel message to his poor parishioners. The clarity and strength of these expressions proceed from the complete identification of poet with singers and reveal a transhistorical comprehension of the oneness of all experience—biblical, contemporary-political, and everyday—as the work of Providence. Both identification and vision suggest the coming of a new age of poetry. In Newton's many failed hymns, which are little more than versified sermonettes exploring a text or analogy in dry, pedantic fashion, he speaks to the singers as a preacher rather than providing for their expressive needs. In these unsuccessful attempts we may discern the passing of the great age of easy didactic verse that had nurtured the young hymn.

William Cowper (1731–1800) brought to his hymn-writing task the accomplished poet's skill and an understanding of genre requirements. Accordingly, his hymns are free of the flaws and confusion that often marred the verse of his predecessors. Watts's visual power, Wesley's exemplary sensibility, and Newton's vitality come together in many of Cowper's sixty-seven hymns. His work enables us to examine more closely the place in hymns of poetic imagination, the "fancy" that had been judged incompatible with hymn purpose. The idiosyncrasies of Cowper's religious understanding, particularly his lack of confidence in either God's loving-kindness or his own salvation, make themselves known in the powerful images he summons up, despite the controls of hymn purpose and convention. The similarities and differences between Cowper's hymns and those of his clergyman predecessors reinforce the conclusions that we have already suggested regarding the special features of the hymn genre and its relationship to romantic poetry.

Metrical Psalms

The evolution of the English hymn reflects the complicated history of the English Reformation. While the initial reform of the English church was essentially Lutheran, the exile of Protestant divines to Calvinist countries during the reign of Mary Tudor changed the course of the movement, which henceforth developed along more Calvinist lines. Luther had appreciated both contemporary German song and the liturgical tradition, but the Reformed church was conscientiously determined to return to the worship practice of the primitive church and accordingly allowed only those items in its service that had clear scriptural precedent.[13] Metrical psalmody was Calvin's gift to England. In 1562 Thomas Sternhold and John Hopkins published their *Whole Book of Psalmes,* the "Old Version," which remained the authoritative church text for more than a century, playing a part in the prehistory of the English hymn that can hardly be exaggerated. It may certainly be anticipated that the kind of church song in universal use, sanctioned by biblical authority and intimately familiar to all worshipers, would provide the paradigm for hymn verse, just as the psalm tunes provided the music. Both the similarities and the differences between hymns and psalms are instructive. This influence of psalms was a constant, as psalms were sung throughout the century. Isaac Watts and Charles Wesley both paraphrased the psalms, a task that they viewed as part of the hymn-writing venture.

The metrical limitations within which the hymn writer worked are an important initial item in the formal description of the hymn as poem. These were the heritage of the metrical psalm. While the number of available tunes, and therefore metrical arrangements, increased radically during the century, in the psalters each psalm was rendered in the three standard measures: common, short, and long. The psalm measures and their hymn use are illustrated as follows.

1. *Common measure* is the psalm version of the ballad stanza, in which four-line stanzas contain lines of eight, six, eight, and six syllables, rhyming ABAB or ABCB.

> I was a grovelling creature once
> And basely cleav'd to earth;
> I wanted spirit to renounce
> The clod that gave me birth.

In common measure, the alternation of long and short lines gives the poet the opportunity to extend the thought and syntactical unit through fourteen syllables, as illustrated by the punctuation of this example. The force of the stanza tends to fall on the longer first and third lines.

2. In psalms and hymns written in *short measure,* the lines contain six, six, eight, and six syllables.

> Ah whither shall I fly?
> I hear the thunder roar;
> The law proclaims destruction nigh
> And vengeance at the door.

In short measure, the short first and second lines lead toward the extended octosyllabic line three, focusing the stanza on a dramatic or rhetorical climax, followed by a short, one-line conclusion, or denouement.

3. In *long measure* each line contains eight syllables and the rhymes are either AABB or ABAB. This English equivalent of the Latin stanza of the Ambrosian hymns is appropriately illustrated by the doxology.

> Praise God from whom all blessings flow,
> Praise Him ye creatures here below,
> Praise Him above, ye heavenly host,
> Praise Father, Son, and Holy Ghost.

The equal length of the eight-syllable lines in long measure affects both the thought, which tends to be confined to the line, and the division into stanzas, which is less rigid.

The metrical options of the early hymn writers were few but distinct in effect. Such formal restrictions were a delight and a challenge to the poetic craftsman.

The rise of the hymn in England has frequently been credited to the inadequacy of the psalter as an expression of modern Christian faith. Both the antique language of Sternhold and Hopkins and the Old Testament, and therefore pre-Christian, content of the psalms are considered to have forced Watts and his fellow hymn writers to forge a practical, Christian alternative. Certainly the apologetic of the hymn writers supports this view. Defending his hymns, Watts wrote: *"David* would have thought it very hard to have been confin'd to the Words of *Moses,* and sung nothing else on all his Rejoycing-days but the *Drowning of* Pharaoh *in the Fifteenth of* Exodus."[14] By extension, a modern David ought not to be confined to the original Davidic verse. John Wesley criticized "the miserable, scandalous doggerel of Hopkins and Sternhold," which he felt his brother's hymns so far surpassed.[15]

When we examine the psalter, this criticism seems extreme. The psalters appear no more rigid or antique than they were impersonal or irrelevant. They are timeless expressions of the human situation in relationship to God. The poetry must have been even more accessible to Isaac Watts's contemporaries, so intimately familiar with the Bible, than it is to "moderns"; and the Christian element was present in the psalms, both by virtue of adaptation and by virtue of traditional readings of the psalms as laden with Christian significance. The need to manufacture hymns of original composition could be explained only partly by the rigidity or innate inadequacy of psalms as church song. Taste in poetry had changed, certainly, between 1562 and 1707, but new translations, like the "New Version" of Tate and Brady, could presumably adjust the psalms to eighteenth-century liking.

A further characteristic of the psalms and their recommended uses, perhaps surprising to readers unfamiliar with these texts, is their subjectivity. Many psalms are highly individual in focus, and it becomes evident that we need not turn to Wordsworth and the romantics for an explanation of the strong feelings found in the young English hymn in the early eighteenth century. In collections of psalms for devotional or congregational use, a careful attempt was made to relate the material to the life of the singer. The French Calvinist precedent is seen in the poem prefaced to *Les Pseaumes de David, mis en rime francoise,* which describes the value of the psalms to the individual religious sensibility:

O gentils cœurs, & ames amoureuses,
S'il en fut onc, quand serez langoureuses
D'infirmité, prison, peché, soucy,
Perte; ou opprobre, arrestez vous icy,
Espece n'est de tribulation,
Qui n'ait icy sa consolation:
C'est un jardin plein d'herbes & racines,
Ou de tous maux se trouvent medecines.[16]

If this preface is any indication, the Old Testament psalms were traditionally appreciated for their primarily individual rather than communal appeal. They were approved and recommended as expressions of personal rather than collective religious sentiment. This private focus deserves examination, and its difference from the function of the later hymn, primarily designed for congregational song, is important.

The prefatory material accompanying Sternhold and Hopkins's version reflects Calvin's contempt for worldly song, that judgment which bound the Reformed tradition to song based safely on Scripture. The psalms are "very mete to be used of all sortes of people privately for their solace & comfort: laying apart all ungodly Songes and Ballades, which tende only to the norishing of vyce, and corrupting of youth." The inclusion in the prefatory material of "A treatise made by Athanasius" on the use of the psalms shows that the practice of matching the various psalms to the believers' various spiritual states was very old indeed: "It is easy therefore for every man to finde out in the Psalmes, the motion and state of his owne soule, and by that meanes, his own figure and proper erudition." Individual psalm prescriptions, taken from Athanasius, illustrate the right use of psalms and their Christian meaning, which had never been seriously questioned:

If thou feelest the threatninges of God, and thereby percevuest thy selfe to be dismaied, thou mayest say the 6. psalm and the .37.

If thou marvelest at th order of thynges created, and the grace of the divine providence syng 19. 26. 27. Psalme.

If thou haste sinned & being turned, fallest to repentance, and wouldest obteyne mercy, thou hast the words of confession in the .51. Psalme.

If thou wilt enstruct anye man in the misterye of the resurrection, thou hast the 80. Psalme.

Such as preache of the divine crosse, and how muche lying in wayte he received for us, and how great things he suffered, are the 2. Psalme, and the 119.

For declaration of his glorious resurrection in the fleshe reade the 24. and the .47. Psalme.

The authors supplement Athanasius with recommendations of their own: "If thou woldest live a godly lyfe, if thou wouldest replenysh thy mynde with goo[d]ly preceptes, and therby obtayne imortalitie, and eternal felicitie: Study diligently the .119. Psalme." The suggested uses of the psalms indicate how they were felt to be comforting, strengthening Christian evangelical tools and sources of truth. Their Christian interpretation and relevance were presumed. Expressing the joys and fears of the faithful individual, they are not exclusively "sung praise." In promoting psalmody, the Calvinists seem to have been fostering a more personal, emotional song than their contemporary Lutherans, whose hymns, in their congregational focus, demand less subjective response and introspection than do the metrical psalms used as directed. This subjectivity and personal focus of psalmody is perhaps unexpected; we might too easily have assumed that "modern" hymns of original composition would be more personal than Old Testament psalms.

The controversy surrounding the translations of the psalter, most notably the relative merits of the Old and New Versions, suggests that the texts of the psalms in English could be, indeed were, altered by the translator to account for changes in poetic idiom as well as in religious perspective. They were far from rigid in shape or content. The place of church officialdom as the approving or disapproving governor of church song is apparent as well in the history of the metrical psalm. A brief comparison of the language of the Old and New Versions will yield information about the trend to which hymns of original composition belong, the purported movement toward more modern, more Christian, more poetic church song.

The first part of Psalm 102 suits our purpose well. In the first stanza, the enhanced subjectivity of the New Version is immediately apparent, as the order of the clauses in the first two lines is changed, throwing emphasis on the singer and the singer's soul rather than on the hearing of the Lord:

O heare my prayer, Lorde, and let,
  my crye come unto thee:
In tyme of troble doo not hide,
  thy face away from me.

When I pour out my Soul in Pray'r,
  Do thou, O Lord, attend:
To thy Eternal Throne of Grace
  Let my sad Cry ascend.

Inclyne thyne eares to me, make haste,
    to heare me when I call:
For as the smoke doth fade, so doo
    my dayes consume and fall.

O hide not thou thy glorious Face
    In times of deep Distress,
Incline thine Eare, and when I call
    My Sorrows soon redress.

Beyond the enhanced personal focus, at the expense of the Lord, the changes in the order of clauses and diction affect lines 3 through 8, "time of trouble" becomes "times of deep Distresse," which reflects the passing of the age of religious martyrdom, perhaps. The anthropomorphic face of the Lord has become the "glorious Face," somewhat removed in its glory, less human. The lofty Eternal Throne of Grace belongs to the New Version, not to the Old, and God's undignified haste is eliminated. The call of the singer is transformed to a "sad cry." The changes, to modern ears, seem to introduce a language and a religious experience that is less immediate. The subjectivity masks a failure in the communication between the singer and the Lord, and the singer is more inclined to turn inward, to contemplate his own feelings.

    A series of similes follows the introductory stanza. The verb comparisons of the old version yield to the less active noun comparisons of the new, while twenty-five lines are drawn out to thirty-one:

(For as the smoke doth fade, so doo
    my dayes consume and fall.)
And as a herth, my bones are burnt:
    my hart is smitten dead,
And withers as the grasse, that I
    forget to eate my bread.
By reason of my groning voyce,
    My bones cleave to my skinne:
As pelicane of wildernes,
    such case now am I in.

And as an oule in desart is,
    loe I am suche a one:
I watch, and as a sparrow on
    the house top am alone.
Loe dayly in reprocheful wise,
    mine enmies doo me scorne
And they that doo against me rage,
    against me they have sworne.

Each cloudy Portion of my Life
    Like scatter'd Smoak expires;
My shriv'led Bones are like a Hearth
    That's parch'd with constant Fires.
My Heart, like Grass that feels the Blast
    Of some infectious Wind,
Is wither'd so with Grief, that scarce
    My needful Food I mind.

By reason of my sad Estate
    I spend my Breath in Groans;
My Flesh is worn away, my Skin
    Scarce hides my starting Bones.
I'm like a Pelican become,
    That does in Desarts mourn;
Or like an Owl that sits all day
    On barren Trees forlorn.

In Watchings or in restless Dreams
    I spend the tedious Night;
Like Sparrows, that on Houses tops
    To sit alone delight.

All day by railing Foes I'm made
   The Object of their Scorn;
Who all, inspir'd with furious Rage,
   Have my Destruction sworn.

Surely with ashes, as with breade,
   my hunger I have filld.
And mingled have my drink with teares
   that fro mine eyes have stild,
Because of thy displeasure, Lord,
   thy wrath and thy disdayne:
For thou has lifted me aloft,
   and cast me downe agayne.

In dust I lie, and all my Bread
   With Ashes mixt appears;
When'er I quench my burning Thirst,
   My Drink is dash'd with Tears.
Because on me with Double weight
   Thy heavy Wrath does lie;
For thou to make my Fall more great
   Didst lift me up on high.

The expansion of the verses was perhaps the result of greater literacy among churchgoers and a wider use of books. When sung without books, psalms and hymns were both "lined out," the assembly repeating the verses, line by line, as they were read by the parish clerk. Lining out forced poetic condensation and avoided enjambment. The New Version is less concise: Tate and Brady tended to modify and qualify nouns—"my dayes" become "each cloudy Portion of my Life"; fading smoke becomes "expiring scatter'd Smoak"; bones become "shriv'led Bones," and line 12 is entirely new. The heart, simply "smitten" in the Old Version, in the New "feels the Blast of some infectious Wind." This diffusion, the noted preference for noun comparisons, and the indulgence in superfluous description do not improve the poetry of the psalms, to either modern or Augustan taste.

In the last stanza of the first part of this psalm, the distinctive features of the new version are revealed most clearly. Indirection, diffusion of imagery, and a specialized "poetic diction" have diluted the verse considerably:

The dayes wherein I pass my lyfe
   are like the fleting shade:
And I am withered like the gras,
   that sone away doth fade,
But thou, O Lord, for ever doest
   remaine in stedy place,
And thy remembrance ever doth
   abide from race to race.

My Days are like the Ev'ning Shade
   That hastily declines.
My Beauty too, like wither'd Grass,
   With faded Lustre pines:
But thy eternal State, O Lord,
   No length of Time shall waste,
The mem'ry of thy wond'rous Works,
   From Age to Age shall last.

The preference for poetic diction is apparent in Tate and Brady's substitution of "the Ev'ning Shade / That hastily declines" for the direct "fleting shade," which is more suggestive and fearful. Immediacy is further lost when "I am withered" yields to "My Beauty too, like wither'd Grass, / With faded Lustre pines." (The withering of the self is a more powerful image than the decay of beauty.) The use of the second-person "thou, O Lord," in Sternhold and Hopkins, is more direct than Tate and Brady's "thy eternal State." Similarly, "thy remembrance" implies a personal familiarity with the Lord that is lacking in "The mem'ry of thy wond'rous Works."

Given the liberties traditionally allowed the translator, the freedom to adapt language and content to both current poetic taste and religious understanding, the biblical psalms may not be seen as rigid texts, an Old Testament prison from which the hymn writers were escaping. Tate and Brady made one of many attempts at modernization. The prescribed uses of the psalms show further that the psalms were accepted as both Christian and expressive of common spiritual states of the believer. The combined characteristics of hymns, suggested in the opening pages of this chapter, provide reasons why a new variety of song was needed.

First of all, while they marvelously expressed a range of familiar spiritual states, the psalms were perhaps insufficiently edifying. If we may draw tentative conclusions from our limited consideration of one part of a single psalm, the expression of desolation in Psalm 102 is faultless. But we have suggested that such expression was not consistent with the didactic aims of the eighteenth-century hymn writers, who wanted to direct expression toward exemplary Christian attitudes, to focus songs on Christian answers, in this case remedies for spiritual desolation. Second, although private use was appropriate, hymns were, by and large, intended for public, congregational singing. The communal setting encouraged a theatrical element in hymnody, seen in the tableaux of Watts, in the dramatic scenes of charismatic conversion of Wesley, and in the stage presence of Newton's preacher-hero, a dramatic inclination often indicated by a call to "Look," "Behold," "See," "Hark," or "Hear." Finally, hymns provided more flexible means of Christian education, the teaching of Bible stories and doctrine, than did psalms. When no coordination whatsoever with biblical texts was required, the writer gained considerable freedom.

Other Models & Precedents

We maintained at the outset of this book that the controlled study of hymns as poetry, written within the traditions of English literature, would yield useful information, of interest beyond the confines of

hymnology, regarding the poetic taste of the century and the religious
convictions of its people. To this end, it is necessary to examine certain
German hymns as a second continuing influence, after the psalms, on
the development of the hymn in England.[17] This is a complex task,
requiring a reversed chronology, as we work back in time from the
well-documented German influence on the Wesley brothers to earlier
importations of German material, of indeterminable influence.

One might expect Luther's famous Reformation hymns to have
served as models for the eighteenth-century hymn writers as they
designed the English hymn, but this was not the case. Both the
language and the attitudes of the sixteenth-century hymns must have
seemed as antiquated to eighteenth-century religious poets as did
those of Sternhold and Hopkins. The trials of religious controversy,
the challenge of the Counter Reformation and of Puritanism, had
intervened, undermining the objectivity of religious experience that
supports the Lutheran hymns (and gave poetic strength and immediacy to the psalms of the Old Version). The Wesleys quite
naturally looked for models among the more recent German hymns,
particularly the hymns of the seventeenth-century Pietists and the
contemporary Moravian Brethren. John Wesley included numerous
translations of Pietist hymns in his first hymnbook, published in
Georgia in 1737.[18]

The Pietist hymns have long been considered part of the heritage
of the Protestant baroque, while the Moravian hymns have hardly
been considered at all. The Protestant baroque, closely related to its
Catholic counterpart, voiced a similar spiritual anxiety coupled with
an often forced concentration on sense experience. A classic example
of Pietist hymnody, in eighteenth-century translation, is Paul Gerhardt's "O Welt! sie hier dein Leben":

> I   Here World see thy Redeemer,
>   Hangs like a curs'd Blasphemer
>   And pants his Life away!
>   The Sov'reign Prince of Glory,
>   Bears like a Lamb before Thee,
>   All th'Hellish Spite of sinful Clay.
>
> II Come near! view well his Bruises,
>   With th'open Crimson Sluices,
>   His Body swims in Blood!
>   His Heart, his Bones and Marrow

   Do melt in Grief and Sorrow,
    As one forsaken of his God.

 III My Life! who is the Author
   Of this unheard of Slaughter?
    Who nail'd Thee to the Cross?
   For Thou art not a Sinner,
   Nor like our Fall's Beginner,
    Whose Offsprings are but hellish Dross.

 IV Lord! I and my Transgressions,
   Have rais'd those cursed Legions
    'Gainst Thee the Prince of Peace!
   These rous'd th'infernal Lion,
   To kill the King of Sion,
    And crucified the Lord of Bliss.

   . . . .

 XIII Thy Scars and Prints so bloody
   I'll make my deepest Study,
    And learn of Thee, my Lamb:
   To bear the worst Affliction,
   And wilful Contradiction,
    Of such as slight Thy glorious Name.[19]

The metrical difference of such a hymn, unbound by the three psalm measures, must have appealed to the Wesleys. How much more were they impressed by the language and imagery? The agony of both Christ and the sinful spectator of the Crucifixion is heightened. The panting, bloody Crucifixion is sharply contrasted to the regal glory of Christ the King, the Lord of Bliss. Human depravity is total, as reflected in the similes "like a curs'd Blasphemer," "as one forsaken of his God," and "nor like our Fall's Beginner," and stated outright in "sinful clay" and "hellish dross." The singer is conducted through a powerful spiritual experience.

It has been said that, in contrast to the hymns of Luther, the baroque hymns "show a more marked personal element, a richer palette of colors, more elaborate imagery, wider use of antithesis, and an intensification of elements of drama and mystery capable of inspiring awe."[20] Here was the answer to the insipidity of Tate and Brady. Both the strong language and the baroque world view of these hymns would seem anachronistic in the Augustan period, particularly if we persist in calling it a neoclassical age, yet these Pietist baroque features are found in many hymns of Watts and Wesley.

Their Moravian friends had introduced the Wesley brothers to the collection of Pietist hymns made by Johann Anastasius Freyling-hausen. The story of the Wesleys' friendship with the Moravians is well known. John learned German in order to talk with the Brethren and maintained friendship with the group in Georgia and later, when he was back in England. He visited Herrnhut, the center of the movement, in 1738. The Moravians were more than intermediaries, however, and they did not simply introduce the Wesleys to Pietist hymns. Their own hymns are unique in the comparative history of hymnology, and they were part of the Wesleyan background.

While many Moravian hymns follow the traditional Lutheran model, the most distinctive carry the bloodiness and grotesquerie of the Pietist hymns to a difficult and unpleasant extreme, an intimate enjoyment of the wounds of Christ. This phenomenon was the literary manifestation of an important hallmark of Moravian doctrine. Rejecting the tortured religious attitude of the Pietists, the painful abjection, they stressed the childlike joy of the Christian, freed from guilt and sin. In their hymns they retained the grotesque language and imagery, of blood and wounds, but in new combination with joyful liberation. The singers addressed Jesus:

> Appear before me evermore
>   In this red mangled Hue!
> And follow me where'er I turn,
>   Still closely me pursue.
> Embrace me fast within Thy Arms,
>   Thou Bridegroom of my Soul,
> And let thy Blood besprinkle me
>   From ev'ry pierced Hole.[21]

The relationship between God and the singer is quite different here from the relationship posited in the Gerhardt hymn. The horrible apparition is at odds with its gentle, loving intention.

A less successful translation of another Moravian hymn illustrates the bizarre extremes to which this inclination could lead. These stanzas on the pleura are from a 1749 collection:

> God's Side-hole, hear my Prayer,
>   Accept my Meditation:
> On thee I cast my Care

With Child-like Adoration.
While Days and Ages pass, and endless periods roll,
An everlasting Blaze shall sparkle from that Hole.

Lovely Side-hole, dearest Side-hole,
Sweetest Side-hole made for me,
O my most beloved Side-hole,
I wish to be lost in thee.
O my dearest Side-hole,
Thou art to my Bride soul,
The most dear and loveliest Place: Pleura's Space!
Soul and Body in thee pass![22]

The affectionate, childlike pleasure in the wound is peculiarly repulsive. It might be suggested that this hymn betrays the translator's insensitivity to appropriate English religious diction, as the translations cling rigidly to the original and ignore the usual standards of English taste.

John Wesley was to attack the Moravian hymns when he became disenchanted with Moravian theology, particularly because the Moravians disagreed with his teaching of perfectability. His attacks on both hymns and doctrine betray his earlier fascination with both. The Moravians' belief in the Christian's liberation from sin and guilt distinguished their theology from that of the Pietists. Wesley overtook them in their own direction and proceeded further than they were willing to. Perhaps John Wesley or his associates had a hand in the 1749 publication of a short collection of Moravian hymns. *Hymns composed for the USE of the Brethren,* "By the Right Reverend, and most illustrious C. Z. Published for the Benefit of all Mankind," betrays its publisher's hostility to the Brethren. The texts are taken from the poorly translated *Collection* of 1749.[23]

The Moravian influence on the Wesley hymn, like the Moravian influence on Wesleyan theology, was manifold. The German group inspired the Wesleys to learn German and exposed them to a variety of German hymns and their use. The Wesleys profited. The Moravians also provided a model for the adaptation of the seventeenth-century hymn to mid-eighteenth-century thought. Charles Wesley was to follow much the same procedure. Finally, by negative example, the Moravians provided a lesson in poor hymn writing, which perhaps served as a warning about the dangers of extravagance and idiosyncrasy in the hymn type.

The art of hymn translation was not as unsophisticated as it appears in the 1749 collection of Moravian hymns, nor was John Wesley the first to import German hymnody into England in the eighteenth century. In 1722, John Christian Jacobi had assembled a book that he titled *Psalmodia Germanica or, a specimen of Divine Hymns, Translated from the High Dutch*. The volume was dedicated to the Hanoverian princesses Anne, Amalia, and Carolina: "The following Sheets exhibit a Translation of *Psalmody*, used in the Native Country of YOUR ROYAL HIGHNESSES, which (as well as other Protestant Countries) is blessed with those Spiritual Hymns, to the frequent Use whereof the Apostle doth so solemnly exhort." Hymns were not sung in Anglican church services, but inasmuch as a German prince sat on the English throne, such a collection with a royal dedication is more than a curiosity. Jacobi's prefatory remarks concerning the exposure of the English people to German hymnody are suggestive of probable influence: "Many of the *British* Nation, having heard the sacred *Psalmody*, us'd in the *German* Congregations at *London*, have wish'd to see the same done into *English*, and set to the same Tunes and Metre wherein they were originally compos'd." If Jacobi may be trusted, the German hymns were known by and appealed to the English as church song—particularly if they were called psalmody rather than hymns, as "hymns" were associated with dissent.

The *Psalmodia Germanica* nevertheless includes two compositions by Isaac Watts, whose work Jacobi felt resembled that of his German colleagues:

I have, with the Leave of the Reverend *Mr. Watts*, transcrib'd one entire Hymn out of his *Horae Lyricae*, upon the Nativity of *Christ*, and the 127 Psalm, out of his new Translation; both which agree so well with our *German* Composures on those Subjects, that I made bold to try, how a good *English* Verse, set to a *German* Tune, might be relish'd by a *British* Singer.

Watts himself had distinguished the poems of the *Horae Lyricae* from the hymns, which he considered properly less imaginative. The psalm paraphrases, as performed by Watts, were closer in purpose and design to his hymns but were distinct nonetheless. Samples of both lyrics and psalms by Watts struck Jacobi as English equivalents of the German hymns. He also saw the advantage of importing German tunes for English compositions, a trend of the future.

We are left with the question as to whether this German sympathy of Watts coincidentally resulted from a common faith, biblical sources, and a common purpose or manifested an actual influence. Watts evidently knew Jacobi and was familiar with his 1722 project, but Watts's hymns were the work of his youth, and any documented association with German divines occurred in later years.[24] We may also consider the likelihood that the younger Watts had heard German hymns sung or had read them in manuscript translation. There were certainly Germans in England in the first decade of the eighteenth century. Even earlier they provide us with a link between the German Pietism of Halle and the English religious societies of the last years of the seventeenth century.

According to Josiah Woodward's *Account of the Rise and Progress of the Religious Societies in the City of London &c And of Endeavors for Reformation of Manners which have been made therein,* the Reverend Anthony Horneck fathered the religious society movement. (The piety cultivated in the societies anticipated the Wesley Holy Club by fifty years and shared many of its principles.) Horneck was born in 1641 and was educated in Germany, served as tutor with the family of the duke of Albemarle, and was preacher at the Savoy for twenty-six years. While Horneck was wholeheartedly Anglican and may well have abandoned the hymns of his youth, his activities remind us that educated piety existed alongside the touted decadence of the Restoration and during the following years, discouraging the view that Watts and his fellows were voices crying in a moral wilderness.[25]

The second figure illustrating the German presence in England is Anthony William Boehm, "chaplain to his Royal Highness, Prince George of Denmark and Minister of the German Chapel at St. James in London." Boehm, born in 1673, was educated at Halle, the center of Pietism. (He was sufficiently radical in his opinions to arouse orthodox opposition in his first position, as tutor in Waldeck.) He went to England in 1710, employed by several German families particularly interested in having a Halle graduate as schoolmaster for their children. He learned English from "two German Students who kept an *English* and *Latin* school" in London and by becoming acquainted with "several Members of the religious Societies." By 1712 he was ready to open a German school in Bedford-Bury, where many German families reportedly lived. Shortly thereafter he was chosen to help Dr. Mecken with the preaching in the prince consort's chapel. Like the Pietist he was, Boehm sang hymns, including those of Paul Gerhardt.[26]

The influence of German Pietist hymns, alongside the seventeenth-century English tradition of devotional lyrics, would help to account for the presence in Watts's hymns of certain seemingly anachronistic elements. Spiritual tension is frequently expressed in startling language and grotesque imagery that contrast sharply with the more general Augustan mood and poetic taste of Watts's hymns. Blood-and-wounds imagery and the divine love model recur, to a lesser degree, in Wesley's hymns and in the Olney collection. No substantial proof of the young Watts's familiarity with German models is available; but if Cowper's "fountain fill'd with blood" and Paul Gerhardt's "open Crimson Sluices" and the blood-and-wounds hymns of the Moravians are in fact related, a new perspective on both hymns and the comparative literary traditions of the eighteenth century becomes possible.[27]

Several hymnologists have puzzled over the worms and bowels and blood in the hymns of the age, unable to account for their strong language and upsetting imagery. G. H. Vallins, in *The Wesleys and the English Language*, wrote: "Certainly the metaphor of the worm, though it suggests and emphasizes humility, is not acceptable to modern Methodists, and does, indeed, lend itself to a certain ludicrousness of imagery."[28] Ernest Rattenbury sought to explain the violent and bloody crucifixions, yielding their violent and bloody atonement, as "Mithraic," locating a characteristic of baroque literature but unable to relate it to its tradition: "An examination of Scripture will show that it is only by straining metaphors out of their normal meaning that any sort of justification can be found for this sort of language. . . . The Old Testament never justifies such expressions as plunging into fountains of blood and the like."[29] We have the advantage of more recent study of seventeenth-century precedents.

The seventeenth-century German hymns and their Moravian successors are not the only possible models for verse we hardly dare to call "baroque." They are significant items within the hymn genre, but English and Latin texts imbued with baroque spirit were available as well. Marc Bertonasco has described the strong Puritan baroque presence in England, particularly evident in the emblem books.[30] This impulse, seemingly at such odds with the central Anglican tradition, is manifest in the poetry of

Crashaw and even Herbert. Watts was impressed by the writing of the Polish Jesuit Mathias Casimire Sarbiewski, and translated some few of his texts from the original Latin. Newton repeatedly calls attention to the emblematic nature of his own images. Such influences from outside the hymn genre are best taken as supportive evidence of a continuity of taste, however modified or adjusted to current expectations, between Gerhardt and Cowper.

❧ II ❧

Isaac Watts's
Divine Delight

In Defense of Hymnody

The acceptance of hymns for congregational use, necessary for the establishment of the hymn tradition, depended on a departure from the principle, formulated by Calvin and upheld by the Reformed churches, that Christian song must confine itself to biblical texts, the proper piety of which was guaranteed by divine revelation. Someone had to write hymns that could overcome this resistance. Ideally the champion of hymns would belong to a denomination unbound by church hierarchy, with its need to be persuaded. He would be a man of irreproachable piety, who would speak with authority of the devotional life. And he would be a competent poet, whose taste and opinions lay within the mainstream, eminently uncontroversial. Supplementing these political requirements, and in line with our preliminary definition of the hymn, the father of the English hymn ought probably to be a clergyman or preacher, familiar with the experiences of his people and comfortable in his role as leader and educator. He had to be able to distinguish between his private fears and vision and the public requirements of his call. Finally, hymn singing was sufficiently revolutionary that the originator had to understand precisely what he was doing and why hymns mattered.

Not surprisingly, Isaac Watts met all these requirements. Minister of the prominent Independent Mark Lane meeting, a popular preacher and educator, and known for his personal piety, Watts wrote with the necessary authority. Watts was a skilled poet, and his religious opinions and literary taste are those of his day. He was well equipped and well motivated to fashion and to defend hymns that were acceptable as sensible supplements to congregational life.[1]

In the preface to his first collection of poetry, the *Horae Lyricae* (1706), Watts attempted to define a place for original poetry in Calvinist religious life. Puritan suspicion of the immorality of literature had to be dealt with and, ideally, reconciled to an equally venerable humanistic-puritan enthusiasm for the constructive possibilities of pious poetry. The prefatory essay is an apologia, advocating a religious literature that might compete with immoral, secular poetry. Watts's less lenient colleagues, he reports, held that "all that arises a Degree above Mr. *Sternhold* is too airy for Worship, and hardly escapes the Sentence of *unclean and abominable.*" [2] With the Bible as the great precedent for religious poetry, Watts found it "strange that Persons that have the Bible in their Hands should be led away by thoughtless Prejudices to so wild and rash an Opinion." The devotional use of the psalms had guaranteed a place for poetry in the lives of all believers; the next challenge was to justify texts unhallowed by the divine revelation that sanctified the Scriptures.

Conforming to Calvinist critical tradition and recalling Sternhold's and Hopkins's strictures against those "ungodly Songes and Ballades, which tende only to the norishing of vyce, and corrupting of Youth," Watts admitted that, in contemporary practice, "the Vices have been painted like so many Goddesses, the Charms of Wit have been added to Debauchery, and the Temptation heightned where Nature needs the strongest Restraint." The poet was surely responsible for the effect of his poetry on the souls of his readers, an ethical responsibility he had failed to accept:

Thus almost in vain have the Throne and the Pulpit cry'd *Reformation,* while the Stage and licentious Poems have waged open War with the pious Design of Church and State. The Press has spread the Poyson far, and scatter'd wide the mortal infection; unthinking Youth have been enticed to Sin beyond the vicious Propensities of Nature, plung'd early into Diseases and Death, and sunk down to Damnation in Multitudes. . . . How will these Allies of the nether World, the lewd and profane Versifyers stand aghast before the great Judge, when the Blood of many Souls whom they never saw shall be laid to the Charge of their Writings, and be dreadfully requir'd at their Hands? The Reverend Mr. *Collier* has set this awful Scene before them in just and flaming Colours. [P. v]

A seemingly strange item in a defense of poetry, such an opinion is not as radical as it may appear: the generally accepted instructive duty of literature has simply been translated from the moral to the religious realm and has been lit with sulphur lamps. The didactic responsibility of the poet, seen through Calvinist eyes, was a life-and-death concern. The poet who was a good teacher would go to heaven, while the poet who neglected his calling and lured his readers into vice would be damned.

The novelty of Watts's view, as we watch it unfold, is that his version of literary morality and religion is attuned to contemporary psychology, which in its historical turn was indebted to the spiritual self-consciousness of the Puritans. The promotion of virtue depended on the poet's capacity to move his reader, to inspire feelings conducive to virtue and piety. This feature is characteristic of the literature not of romance but of sensibility. Religious feeling was good in itself, a hallmark of piety, and good as well as a motive force, encouraging virtuous living.

The new element lightens the poet's heavy burden of responsibility and renders an honest enjoyment of literature legitimate. Indeed, Watts's love of literature rings in the language of his protest against the immorality of contemporary literary practice. Joy in words was not new to religion; good preaching demands verbal wit and a rhetorical ear. The understanding of how imaginative literature might function as a means to a devotional end was, however, distinct from traditional understanding. Virtuous poetry elevated thoughts and inspired piety. Dramatic literature was particularly effective, and Watts delighted in the pious effects of French tragedy: "What a Variety of Divine Scenes are display'd, and pious Passions awaken'd in those Poems? The Martyrdom of *Polyeucte,* how doth it reign over our Love and Pity, and at the same time animate our Zeal and Devotion!" (p. xii). Love and pity, the accepted audience responses to tragedy, become means to a religious end. Such a transformation of Horatian aesthetics was made possible by an emphasis on religious feelings as both manifestations of and spurs to piety.

Watts suggested in his preface that Christianity contained much unexploited literary ground, promising the developer greater rewards than classical mythology or heroic legend: "The Heaven and the Hell in our Divinity are infinitely more delightful and dreadful than the Childish Figments of a Dog with three Heads, the Buckets of the *Belides,* the Furies with snaky Hairs, or all the flowry Stories of *Elysium*" (pp. xiii–xiv). The great poet, "employ'd in dressing the

Scenes of Religion in their proper Figures of Majesty, Sweetness and Terror," could win over the world. Watts's feeling for dramatic effects was a salient characteristic of his hymns, employed to inspire efficacious dread and delight.

The idealized figure of the Christian poet might remind us of Milton, but the contrast between the two figures is more instructive. Milton's epic task, his famous justification of the ways of God, is in the classical, Renaissance tradition. The same cannot be said of Watts, who wanted "to diffuse Virtue, and allure Souls to God." The new age of Locke, Shaftesbury, and sentimental morality demanded a different approach. Christian heroism was possible in Milton's frame; exemplary sensibility and intelligent piety were the equivalents in Watts's world. That the two men represented very different ages in taste as well is apparent from Watts's failure to appreciate Milton's poetic idiom.[3] The worlds of their experience were different. The political and religious crises of the seventeenth century had passed, leaving religious thinkers with the obligation to find new bearings, independent of the larger world stage. Watts's hymns are still in general use, while Milton's far greater achievement is, no doubt unfortunately, consigned to courses in the history of British literature.

In his preface to *Hymns and Spiritual Songs* (1707), Watts explained the difference between his hymns and the earlier poems of the *Horae Lyricae*. His explanation of this difference between the two varieties of religious verse recalls the main points of the earlier preface. Verses showing "boldness" or "fancy," by virtue of their daring, had become odes and had been removed. In these rejected odes, the poet had discovered expressions unsuitable for use by common people of common faith, a judgment betraying the familiar concern about the moral dangers of literary expression.[4] Given the undeniable presence of boldness and fancy in the hymns, Watts was probably preempting criticism by readers hostile to hymns of modern composition, allaying their fears.[5]

In his preface, Watts constructed a double defense of his hymns that helps us grasp the apologetic task. Calling the hymns "poems" and "odes," he appealed to the literary reader to excuse his failings as a poet, as his aims had been devotional. In the next breath, he confessed to the pious critic that he had sometimes been lured from his devotional purpose by the attractions of poetry:

If there be any Poems in the Book that are capable of giving Delight to Persons of a more refin'd Taste and polite Education, perhaps they may be found in this Part [the hymns of original composition]; but except they lay aside the Humour of Criticism, and enter into a devout Frame, every Ode here already despairs of pleasing. I confess my self to have been too often tempted away from the more Spiritual Designs I propos'd, by some gay and flowry Expressions that gratify'd the Fancy; the bright Images too often prevail'd above the Fire of Divine Affection; and the Light exceeded the Heat. [P. lv]

Watts was apparently trying to justify his hymns to two different audiences, the stringent Puritans and the independent literati. But we miss an important feature of his work if we fail to appreciate how genuinely he was torn between the call to retreat from an evil world and the delights of the fancy. In the earlier preface he had shared the moral concern of the more rigorous believers at the same time that he delighted in the literary imagination and its pious possibilities. The conflicting claims of pious austerity and poetry are one manifestation of the double call to both self-denial and "Divine Delight," to asceticism and to joy, that spurred Watts's interest in writing hymns. He acknowledged that the ascetic view of an otherworldly and austere spirituality was legitimate, yet he knew that poetry depends for its substance, and even more importantly, for any constructive effect, on its tangible, worldly resources, including literary pleasure.

Hymn singing should be pleasant. Hymns "should elevate us to the most delightful and divine Sensations," helping to "compose our Spirits to Seriousness, and allure us to a sweet Retirement within our selves." This is an answer, decidedly nonascetic and even self-indulgent, to those Christians, including Watts himself, in his more somber frame of mind, who refuse to delight in piety. Such pious pleasure is close in spirit to the attractions of secular virtue described by moralists contemporary with Watts, including Shaftesbury.

Watts described the method he had used in stimulating the desirable delight:

The most frequent Tempers and Changes of our Spirit, and Conditions of our Life are here copied, and the Breathings of our Piety exprest according to the variety of our Passions, our Love, our Fear, our Hope, our Desire, our Sorrow, our Wonder and our Joy, as they are refin'd into Devotion, and act under the Influence and Conduct of the Blessed Spirit. [P. liii]

Watts provided poetic expression for familiar states of mind shared by all believers and, as he articulated such feelings, clarified the correct devotional attitude. He took the singers and their feelings by the hand and led them along an instructive pathway. He intended to stimulate righteous Christian sentiment in much the same way that the dramatist stimulated admiration and pity. The desired end of a hymn thus became the education of religious sensibility by means of the supervised refinement of human feeling into devotional response, with the help of the Blessed Spirit. The focus of the hymn is, ultimately, the individual singer and his or her spiritual progress. Humane understanding, clear devotional purpose, and poetic skill were called for. One's personal struggles and visions were relevant only insofar as they were representative and were controlled by didactic purpose.

An intriguing complex of convictions is manifest in the Christian poetic apologia of the combined prefaces. Watts appears to our modern eyes to have been profoundly eclectic, although there is no evidence that he himself felt that his opinions were incompatible with one another. He fervently and eloquently disapproved of "immoral" worldly literature but drew a distinction between such damnable stuff and uplifting, inspiring, righteous poetry. He wrote that the temptations of the fancy were at odds with spiritual design but affirmed the devotional place of seemingly secular passions. This double vision is combined with a distinctly eighteenth-century view of literary moral purpose and affective-didactic method. Readers, or singers, were to be moved toward virtuous understanding, in this case devotional response, by means of the manipulated reactions to affecting scenes. The supposition behind this method was that the individual was intrinsically capable of virtue or piety. He or she had the resources, which only needed focus and cultivation. This confidence in human ameliorability is apparently at odds with the conviction of the wormlike baseness of humankind. The depravity of humanity, an item of Watts's faith, is evidently incompatible with his poetic intent and method.[6]

The pursuit of these aims and deployment of these methods are controlled, in the end, by the more general requirements of the hymn as congregational song. The feelings expressed in the hymns must be the familiar, "frequent Tempers and Changes of our Spirit and Conditions of our Life." They must be directed by devotional purpose, and they must reach out to the "weaker Christians," involving them in the process of spiritual development and pious understanding.

Watts's skill as a poet and his understanding of his chosen genre were such that his hymns won acceptance in nonconforming churches of his day, served as models for subsequent generations of hymn writers, and are still sung today. Like all permanent literature, the hymns are a product of literary and religious history, appearing at a moment in that history when conditions permitted them to touch human experience of all time. In this connection, Watts's double allegiance, to an otherworldliness that distrusted fanciful flight and idiosyncratic expression and to the devotional and educational possibilities of hymns as poetry, deserves our particular attention.

Instructive Delight

Watts frequently expressed an appreciation of dramatic literature. While his attitude is perhaps surprising in a Calvinist—the Puritans had closed the theaters in the preceding century and Watts had written of the "open War" between stage and pulpit—the dramatic qualities of his hymns provide an important clue to Watts's hymn method. Like drama, hymns are a public genre, dependent for their survival on their broad appeal. They must reach out to capture the attention and involve the interest of the audience-congregation. Like drama, they depend on extraliterary factors, including music. The suitability of religious verse as congregational song and the stage-worthiness of a play are both determined by the author's mastery of his audience and his resources. Watts's special place as innovator in the history of the hymn and his dramatic bent seem to be related: in later years, after hymns were accepted by everybody as a matter of course, adherence to these requirements seems to have become less important.[7]

The entertainment provided by the hymns (as well as by sermons and stained glass windows) is one aspect of "Divine Delight" and at the same time a practical matter of holding audience attention while the verse drives home its point. Visual clarity as an essential means to a didactic end is illustrated by Watts's hymn describing God the Thunderer:

> His Nostrils breathe out fiery Streams,
> And from his awful Tongue
> A Sovereign Voice divides the Flames,
> And Thunder roars along. [LXII, 3]

The draconic heat and noise of God are startling, vaguely pagan. We are brought in close to the enormous divine nostrils and tongue, while the overwhelming fire and thunder impress us with the scale, power, and motion of the vision of God. Description like this provided a kind of entertainment, certainly, while it stocked the minds of the singers with memorable pictures. The instructive vision is of an anthropomorphic deity of tremendous, fearsome power, to whom we must respond with awe, the desirable devotional end of this particular stanza.

While the prefaces may prepare the reader for somewhat tedious hymns, sentimental in the pejorative sense, in fact, the double obligation of the poet to instruct and delight his singers led Watts to write with great daring: the vital, salvific importance of the good passions demanded poetry that played upon them.[8] Certainly this inclination to visualize and even to perform the matter of faith was not unprecedented, either in Catholic or in Protestant tradition, and the biblical history of humanity from Creation to Last Judgment had been dramatic enough to provoke the rebirth of Western drama within the church. Watts's dramatic imagination operated similarly. The Puritan objection to images of God is defied in the best interest of devotional inspiration.

Watts's inclination to paint little scenes and to create little plays may be demonstrated in his handling of three categories of subject matter: (1) necessarily visionary description of God and heavenly affairs; (2) Bible stories; and (3) aspects of Christian experience in this world. Overlap is inevitable, but certain features of each kind are distinguishable, and each has its own challenges for the hymn writer. These religious entertainments all include emotional responses, written into the scenes, in keeping with Watts's devotional-didactic aims. The presence of these exemplary responses points to the most important difference between conventional theatrical entertainment and the hymn counterpart. The singers of hymns play the roles for their own delight and edification. They describe the setting, recite the lines, and respond feelingly, all at once, learning each step of the way. This

variety of experimental theater is illustrated in the visionary hymn
XCI, in which the heavenly curtain rises on an enormous tableau of
the glorified Christ:

1   O the Delights, the heavenly Joys,
        The Glories of the Place
    Where *Jesus* sheds the brightest Beams
        Of his O'er-flowing Grace!

2   Sweet Majesty and awful Love
        Sit smiling on his Brow,
    And all the glorious Ranks above
        At humble Distance bow.

3   Princes to his Imperial Name
        Bend their bright Scepters down,
    Dominions, Thrones, and Powers rejoyce
        To see him wear the Crown.

4   Archangels sound his lofty Praise
        Thro' every heavenly Street,
    And lay their highest Honours down
        Submissive at his Feet.

5   Those soft, those blessed Feet of his
        That once rude Iron tore,
    High on a Throne of Light they stand,
        And all the Saints adore.

6   His Head, the dear Majestick Head
        That cruel Thorns did wound,
    See what Immortal Glories shine,
        And circle it around.

The hymn begins with a quite unextraordinary exclamation of how
wonderful heaven is, followed by an indecipherable if suggestive
image of beams of light being shed and overflowing Grace. Watts's
starting point, in theory and practice, is the commonplace perception
of the believer. He proceeds to expand and refine this vague idea,
leading the spiritual way. To this end, in this hymn, he details an
impressive vision of imperial ranks and all the saints, bowing before
the glorified Christ. The tableau is not cold or austere; we are not
meant to remain distanced or indifferent. Our response is implicit in
the scene painting, a combination of awe and kindly love, summarized
in the rhetorical effect of "Sweet majesty and awful Love," as we are

both lovingly drawn and respectfully put off by what we see. The double response is sustained as stanzas 3 and 4 awe us with the majesty of the important worshipers, all humbled before Jesus, and then as 5 and 6 detail, at close range, the wounds of Jesus and our feeling response to their softness and dearness. The descriptive achievement is such that by the sixth stanza the singers claim to "See" the vision together, having presumably come to understand, by means of the poetry, both Christ's glory and Christ's accessibility.

The collective-expressive starting point of Watts's hymns and his use of dramatic description for his devotional purpose are further demonstrated in hymn XXVI. While universally problematic, the distant inaccessibility of God was a particular challenge of the rational deism of Watts's day. Accordingly, we begin this hymn by articulating our common sense of inferiority and distance from God:

> 1 Lord, we are blind, we Mortals blind,
>   We can't behold thy bright Abode;
>   O 'tis beyond a Creature-Mind,
>   To glance a Thought half way to God.

Despite this common blindness and human mental disability, Watts proceeds, stanza by stanza, to spread before his singers a memorable vision of God as kind and concerned and as imaginatively visible in human form, sitting on a throne, walking on feet, looking with eyes. Our thoughts do indeed glance more than halfway to God:

> 2 Infinite Leagues beyond the Sky
>   The Great Eternal reigns alone,
>   Where neither Wings nor Souls can fly,
>   Nor Angels climb the topless Throne.

> 3 The Lord of Glory builds his Seat
>   Of Gems insufferably bright,
>   And lays beneath his sacred Feet
>   Substantial Beams of gloomy Night.

The devotional process of this hymn consists of imaginatively transcending the singers' inability to see (blindness and vision taken as the central metaphors of the hymn), by means of a detailed vision of God in heaven. The memorable spectacle of the blinding brilliance of the throne and the substantial beams of gloomy Night, trodden down,

bent back by a terrific weight, once more shows the seamless joining
of visual appeal and devotional lesson. The last stanza summarizes
our transformed response:

> 4   Yet, glorious Lord, thy gracious Eyes
>   Look thro', and chear us from above;
>   Beyond our Praise thy Grandeur flies,
>   Yet we adore, and yet we love.

Distance and blindness have been overcome by both new poetic vision
and divine concern.[9]

The second dramatic type, hymns portraying events of biblical record,
is most common in the first book of *Hymns and Spiritual Songs,* which
claims to paraphrase the Scriptures. (Many "hymns of original composition" as well as hymns for communion use are also biblical.) Watts took
great liberties in his adaptations of Bible text to hymn purpose. The first
hymn of book III is a dramatically heightened description of the Last
Supper:

> 1   'Twas on that dark, that doleful Night
>   When Powers of Earth and Hell arose
>   Against the Son of God's Delight,
>   And Friends betray'd him to his Foes:
>
> 2   Before the mournful Scene began
>   He took the Bread, and blest, and brake:
>   What Love thro' all his Actions ran!
>   What wond'rous Words of Grace he spake!

Calling the betrayal a "mournful Scene," Watts indicated just how
consciously he saw the Gospel in visual-dramatic units. He has
heightened the effects, the dark night and the risen powers of earth
and hell, for his purpose. The dramatization is broken by exclamations
defining the singers' appropriate reaction, in this case wonder at
Christ's love in action and grace in word.

In his pursuit of affective impact, Watts did not stop with the
descriptive heightening of atmosphere. He put words in the Lord's
mouth, going well beyond the simple rebellion against Calvin's
insistence that congregational song come from Scripture. Watts's
commitment to the evangelical place of hymns took precedence, and
he daringly wrote new words for Jesus:

7   "Justice unsheath'd its fiery Sword,
        And plung'd it in my Heart:
    Infinite Pangs for you I bore,
        And most tormenting Smart.

8   "When Hell and all its spiteful Powers
        Stood dreadful in my Way,
    To rescue those dear Lives of yours
        I gave my own away.

9   "But while I bled, and groan'd and dy'd,
        I ruin'd *Satan*'s Throne,
    High on my Cross I hung, and spy'd
        The Monster tumbling down." [III, XXI]

This long speech is like a dramatic monologue or operatic recitative. Such sustained discourse strikes us as certainly unsuitable for normal congregational singing unless, in the practice of lining out, when the clerk's voice introduced each line, the incongruity was overcome. The sketch includes the fearful personifications of Justice, Hell, and the Monster and a Christ who is inclined to dwell rather oppressively on his discomforts. The violent activity of these three stanzas is conveyed in the verbs: unsheathe, plunge, bear, torment, rescue, bleed, groan, die, ruin, hang, tumble. Jesus has become the narrator-hero of a fast-moving adventure story, a story designed to drive home the implications of the Passion.

Watts's hymn version of the creation of humanity is similarly dynamic. The poet's imaginative amplification of the Bible text and the commands of the Creator show his familiarity with the discovery of the circulatory system:

He spoke, and strait our Hearts and Brains
    In all their Motions rose;
Let Blood, said he, *flow round the Veins,*
    And round the Veins it flows. [XIX, 5]

The tangible, visible, and audible qualities of such a creation are as remarkable as the fact that Watts dared to write a script for God. The achievement anticipates Hollywood's biblical spectaculars.

After the divine visionary hymns and the Bible story hymns, the third dramatic category is Christian experience in this world, a subject that seems to suit Watts's stated method best. Common experience is more easily manipulated for devotional stimulus than are heavenly visions or Bible stories, particularly since the Bible's narratives are virtually unsurpassable as literature. Indeed, the drama of the Christian life in and after this world had prompted the development of the morality plays in the Middle Ages.

In hymn LII a scene within a scene unfolds. The initial observation is common enough: the godless are in trouble when they die. The dramatic sketch begins with the female personification of the soul, evicted from this life. Her vain appeal, her chains, and the coming misery as one of the damned are the stuff of pathetic tragedy, transmuted by design to inspire our devotion.

> 1   Death! 'Tis a melancholy Day
>   To those that have no God,
>   When the poor Soul is forc'd away
>   To seek her last Abode.
>
> 2   In vain to Heaven she lifts her Eyes,
>   But Guilt, a heavy Chain,
>   Still drags her downward from the Skies
>   To Darkness, Fire, and Pain.

This little scene inspires the singers to ask all hell-bound sinners to mourn their dire situation and to contemplate the pit, which ghastly view leads the saved to sing:

> 3   Awake and mourn ye Heirs of Hell,
>   Let stubborn Sinners fear,
>   You must be driv'n from Earth, and dwell
>   A long *For-ever* there.
>
> 4   See how the Pit gapes wide for you,
>   And flashes in your Face,
>   And thou, my Soul, look downwards too,
>   And sing recovering Grace.

The complex and shifting address of this hymn reflects its multiple purpose as the singer exclaims, narrates, exhorts the hell-bound sinners, and finally speaks to himself or herself. We are encouraged to respond with pity, horror, superiority, worry, and grateful security.

In the context of this life-and-death drama, the doctrine of the elect is explicated.[10]

The deathbed was the dramatic climax of the Christian's life on earth and a useful object of contemplation for those awaiting the day. Watts acknowledged our natural resistance to such morbid thoughts as he gently called our attention to his subject:

> 1   Stoop down, my Thoughts, that use to rise,
>   Converse a while with Death:
>   Think how a gasping Mortal lies,
>   And pants away his Breath.
>
> 2   His quiv'ring Lip hangs feebly down,
>   His Pulses faint and few,
>   Then speechless with a doleful Groan
>   He bids the World adieu. [XXVIII]

Death is acted out in a familiar deathbed scene by a representative mortal, whose lips, pulse, and groan we see, feel, and hear. In the interest of our devotion, our concentration on our own mortality, death is put before us naturalistically.

While such specific, very real Death is everpresent ("The Moment when our Lives begin / We all begin to die" [LVIII]), so are the comforting qualities, and the figures of Mercy, Love, Goodness, and Grace arrange themselves in a memorable tableau of the divine attributes:

> 5   'Tis Sovereign Mercy finds us Food,
>   And we are cloath'd with Love:
>   While Grace stands pointing out the Road,
>   That leads our Souls above.
>
> 6   His Goodness runs an endless Round;
>   All Glory to the Lord:
>   His Mercy never knows a Bound;
>   And be his Name ador'd.

The echo of Spenser and the morality plays is as remarkable as the anticipation of Blake. Traditional personifications, like traditional contemplation of the deathbed, suited Watts's poetic purpose.

The contrast between present pain and future delight, necessary and instructive to the suffering believer, is the substance of the famous hymn "A Prospect of Heaven makes Death easy" (LXVI):

1   There is a Land of pure Delight
       Where Saints Immortal reign;
    Infinite Day excludes the Night,
       And Pleasures banish Pain.

2   There everlasting Spring abides,
       And never-withering Flowers:
    Death like a narrow Sea divides
       This Heav'nly Land from ours.

3   Sweet Fields beyond the swelling Flood
       Stand drest in living Green:
    So to the *Jews* Old *Canaan* stood,
       While *Jordan* roll'd between.

4   But timorous Mortals start and shrink
       To cross the narrow Sea,
    And linger shivering on the Brink,
       And fear to lanch away.

5   O could we make our Doubts remove,
       These gloomy Doubts that rise,
    And see the *Canaan* that we love,
       With unbeclouded Eyes.

6   Could we but climb where *Moses* stood,
       And view the Landskip o're,
    Not *Jordan's* Stream, nor Death's cold Flood,
       Should fright us from the Shore.

The hymn develops in the established pattern. The first two lines voice our common, nonspecific understanding of heaven. The following four lines detail heaven, contrasting heavenly pleasure, springtime, and absence of decay with their familiar earthly shadows. Stanza 3 introduces the parallel of the Promised Land. The descriptive stage thus set, in stanza 4 we view a crowd of shivering people, deathly afraid. In stanzas 5 and 6 we have become those mortals, our vision obscured because we lack Moses' perspective. Drawing on the familiar Old Testament story, Watts has used descriptive and dramatic resources to move his singers toward an understanding of life in its eternal context. The message is familiar; the formulation is new—a function of the demands of the hymn genre to begin with common feeling or perception, to entertain, and to teach.

Almost every Watts hymn contains a little dramatic scene or the sketch for a religious painting. The devil's methods are demonstrated in CLVI, perhaps inadvertently demonstrating those temptations of fancy that Watts acknowledged had threatened him as well:

1 I hate the Tempter and his Charms,
  I hate his flatt'ring Breath;
  The Serpent takes a thousand Forms
   To cheat our Souls to Death.

2 He feeds our Hopes with airy Dreams,
  Or kills with slavish Fear;
  And holds us still in wide Extreams,
   Presumption, or Despair.

3 Now he perswades, *how easy 'tis*
  To walk the Road to Heav'n;
  Anon he swells our Sins, and crys,
   They cannot be forgiv'n:

4 He bids young Sinners, *Yet forbear*
  To think of God or Death;
  For Prayer and Devotion are
   But melancholy Breath.

5 He tells the Aged, *They must die,*
  And 'tis too late to pray;
  In vain for Mercy now they cry,
   For they have lost their Day.

6 Thus He supports his cruel Throne
  By Mischief and Deceit;
  And drags the Sons of *Adam* down
   To Darkness and the Pit.

7 Almighty God, cut short his Power,
  Let him in Darkness dwell:
  And, that he vex the Earth no more,
   Confine him down to Hell.

The hatred of the first line is simple enough as a starting position, followed by seven lines summarizing satanic methods. Stanzas 3 through 5 then require the singers to speak the Tempter's lines, playing an apparently odd part in their own dramatic lesson. The recitation of satanic arguments is instructive, but given Watts's usual control of dramatic effects, it is likely that he intended much more.

The general hatred of the Tempter is transformed into a more thorough repulsion by these dramatic means. The satanic lines, which are really supremely unsuitable for church song, are meant to revolt the singers. They are indeed more gripping than the generalizations of the opening stanzas. Watts designed these three stanzas as a lively demonstration of the dangers at hand: thus Satan manages to deceive. We are collectively relieved when the Almighty God's power is finally manifest in the last stanza.

By his own account and as seen in the hymns, Watts's ability to dramatize and visualize his material was always subordinated to the cause of devotional education. In the dramatic hymns his pattern was to orient the singers in the opening lines by articulating the simplest truth, then to build a hymn that broadened the singers' consciousness and explored the implications of that truth, often by means of vignettes of heaven, biblical events, or familiar experiences. While the homiletic model is apparent, the hymn was not a sermon, with an authoritative exposition to be passively heeded, but a participatory poetic genre. The people were to sing the description, the complaints of Jesus, God's lines at the Creation, and the Tempter's lies. As poetry, the hymns employ linguistic coloring and metaphorical suggestion that help us to appreciate Watts's poetic resources and his public's taste. As participatory literature, they are filled with indicators of the response to his subjects that Watts felt to be right and natural. Identification of these devotional responsive goals aids us in our effort to clarify the religious world view of Watts and the place of the hymns within it.[11]

Devotional Response

The verse pictures of Watts's hymns are frequently violent, bloody, and contorted in the manner of Paul Gerhardt. While the presence of such strong visual elements is indisputable, these hymns distinguish themselves from their Pietist counterparts and from seventeenth-century English prototypes by their greater degree of affective self-consciousness. The envisioned torments press the singers toward a personal melting, partly mystical, partly the manifestation of extreme sensibility. The best example of this distinctive use of traditional imagery is Watts's most popular hymn:

1   When I survey the wond'rous Cross
    On which the Prince of Glory dy'd,
    My richest Gain I count but Loss,
    And pour Contempt on all my Pride.

2   Forbid it, Lord, that I should boast
    Save in the Death of *Christ* my God;
    All the vain things that charm me most,
    I sacrifice them to his Blood.

3   See from his Head, his Hands, his Feet,
    Sorrow and Love flow mingled down;
    Did e're such Love and Sorrow meet?
    Or Thorns compose so rich a Crown?

4   His dying Crimson like a Robe
    Spreads o're his Body on the Tree,
    Then am I dead to all the Globe,
    And all the Globe is dead to me.

5   Were the whole Realm of Nature mine,
    That were a Present far to small;
    Love so amazing, so divine
    Demands my Soul, my Life, my All. [III,VII]

The subject of this hymn is established in the first stanza as the moral effect on the singer of viewing the cross. In the exemplary response, possessions and pride are reduced by the cross to mere loss and contempt. The reordering of the viewer-singer's values is continued in the sacrifice of vanities to the sacrificed blood. After this careful preparation for the actual Crucifixion, the curtain rises in the fourth and fifth stanzas on a fine example of Watts's descriptive drama in which the physical violence of the Crucifixion is heightened and exaggerated by the use of strong metaphor.

One might be inclined to argue that the flowing wounds in the third stanza and the robe of crimson in the fourth are not meant to be visualized, that they are conventional Christian images, not intended to startle or to bother the mind's eye. The injunction to "See" and the vividly pictorial quality of Watts's other hymns indicate the contrary. Any dilution of the power of the imagery results not from its conventionality but rather from the author's call to intersperse devotional instruction to the singers. In stanza 3, for example, the rhetorical questions hone the singers' feelings rather than clarifying the vision of the cross, while in stanza 4 the stress falls on our death to the world rather than on the bloody death of Jesus.

Obvious seventeenth-century influences aside, the calculated effects of many of Watts's hymns seem to proceed from a new variety of spiritual stress. The disparity between sinners and their heavenly context, between our nature as depraved worms and the distant realms of glory, is extremely difficult to handle, devotionally or theologically. In XXVI, which began "Lord we are blind," God was "the Great Eternal," reigning alone, "Infinite Leagues beyond the Sky," a deistic God, not an involved, possibly wrathful Father. This distant abstractness is further described in hymn LXVII and is contrasted with an exclamation about our human depravity. The absolute contrast affects the image of the following two lines, and we envision a collection of ignoble animals, bowing before and offering their praises to, a faraway deity:

> Great God, how Infinite art Thou!
>   What worthless Worms are we!
> Let the whole Race of Creatures bow,
>   And pay their Praise to thee.

In stanza 5, the contrast between the human and the divine is expanded:

> Our Lives thro' various Scenes are drawn,
>   And vex'd with trifling Cares;
> While thine Eternal Thought moves on
>   Thine undisturb'd Affairs.

Our little human world of transitory pretend experience and inconsequential problems is as nothing to God. The suggestion of divine indifference is unavoidable.

Professor Wellek has suggested that the tension between Counter Reformation otherworldliness and Renaissance spirit produced typical baroque literature.[12] We seem to have located a later, parallel tension, in which a similar literary stress derives from the combination of an enlightened, philosophically glorious prime mover and a depraved, wormlike humanity. The two pictures, one of an indifferent, removed divinity, the other of a guilty and vile mankind, are not basically compatible. The god of the deists was the god of "reasonable" people, who found the world as they experienced it an orderly and pleasant place, or at least capable of improvement. The god of the Calvinists was traditionally anthropomorphic, capable of love and wrath and selectivity. Watts's use of strong description indicates that one way to force contact between the distant god and bestial man was by violent metaphor. The Christian can triumph over flesh and sense and "find" God only by focusing on the fleshly and physical nature of the Passion. This becomes an exaggerated emphasis on the very orthodox turn to Christ as mediator between God and man, the incarnation bridging the abyss between divine expectations and sinful human nature. The physical reality of flesh and blood, pain and death, even taken to violent and morbid extremes, jolts the singers by physical means into spiritual awareness and feeling response.

The "dear Flesh" of Jesus left "a long Perfume" in the Tomb (III). The blood imagery of the Bible is exploded as we are over and again "bath'd in blood" from the "open'd Veins" of Christ. The redeeming blood becomes a sea in which we drown (LXXXV). One's heart is a rock, in a crimson sea, a "Bath of Blood Divine" (XCVIII). The wounds of Christ are the source of a healing fountain, "springing from the Veins of Jesus" (III, XXII). The exaggerated bloodiness, the concentration on death and dying, and the images of the depraved nature of humanity combine in the Communion hymns, when "Th' Eternal God comes down and bleeds / To nourish dying Worms" (III, XVII). Watts's dramatic and visual method forces us to picture the scene, and we join in the banquet, at which we consume "dainties" and eat good food.

The devouring of sacred flesh becomes grotesque as the paradox of Jesus as both host and meat is explored:

1 *Jesus,* we bow before thy Feet,
   Thy Table is divinely stor'd:
   Thy Sacred Flesh our Souls have eat,
   'Tis living Bread; we thank thee, Lord!

2 And here we drink our Saviour's Blood,
   We thank thee, Lord, 'tis generous Wine;
   Mingled with Love the Fountain flow'd
   From that dear bleeding Heart of thine.

3   On Earth is no such Sweetness found,
     For the Lamb's Flesh is heav'nly Food;
     In vain we search the Globe around
     For Bread so fine or Wine so good.

4   Carnal Provisions can at best
     But cheer the Heart or warm the Head,
     But the rich Cordial that we taste
     Gives Life Eternal to the Dead.

5   Joy to the Master of the Feast,
     His Name our Souls for ever bless:
     To God the King and God the Priest
     A loud *Hosanna* round the Place. [III, XVIII]

The communicant speaks like a gourmand, pleased with the exceptional fare. But the bread is the flesh (not the body, which would be less disturbing) of the master of the feast, to whom the hymn is addressed, and the wine has come gushing from his heart (and a fountain of blood is a violent picture indeed). The startling combination of the sacramental imagery of living bread and realistic reference to everyday dining reveals Watts's method in one of its most extreme forms. While the poetic means are radical, the didactic yield is perfectly unextraordinary.

Violent imagery was one way of forcing together godly and worldly experience, of bringing sedate, conventional metaphors to devotional life. An alternative solution to the problem, one more generally sanctioned in both Christian and other religious tradition, is ascetic withdrawal from the concerns of this world. The implication of this approach is that we can in fact purify ourselves by disengagement from mundane preoccupations; the world is contaminated, but we ourselves are salvageable. Collective humanity is depraved, but private piety is attainable as an individual, interior achievement. We are not called to particular charitable works or to neighborly concern. We must rather tune out all the noise of earth that drowns out the voice of the spirit. Watts helps us to cultivate such asceticism with his hymns:

1   My God, permit me not to be
     A Stranger to my Self and Thee;
     Amidst a thousand Thoughts I rove
     Forgetful of my highest Love.

2 Why should my Passions mix with Earth,
   And thus debase my heavenly Birth?
   Why should I cleave to things below,
   And let my God, my Saviour go?

3 Call me away from Flesh and Sense,
   One Sovereign Word can draw me thence;
   I would obey the Voice Divine,
   And all inferiour Joys resign.

4 Be Earth with all her Scenes withdrawn,
   Let Noise and Vanity be gone;
   In secret Silence of the Mind
   My Heav'n, and there my God I find. [CXXII]

The private focus is generalized by virtue of its collective expression, and the singers practice parallel inward turnings. This heaven and the God of the secret silence of the mind is one solution to the problem of locating God and relating him to human life, a solution with implications for our understanding of devotional attitude in Watts's other hymns.

Watts's use of personal, familiar, human experience and casual language is characteristic of both the "violent" hymns and the more ascetic hymns. In the former, the dramatic subject is not framed or distanced but rather intermingles with the everyday experiences, like dining, of the reader or the congregation. In the ascetic hymns, the pleasures and pains of common life are recalled for purposes of comparison and contrast. In a homely medical simile, the wretched cravings of earthly life are compared to feverish insomnia and thirst:

1 Man has a Soul of vast Desires,
   He burns within with restless Fires,
   Tost to and fro his Passions fly
   From Vanity to Vanity.

2 In vain on Earth we hope to find
   Some solid Good to fill the Mind,
   We try new Pleasures, but we feel
   The inward Thirst and Torment still.

3 So when a raging Fever burns
   We shift from side to side by turns,

> And 'tis a poor Relief we gain
> To change the Place but keep the Pain.
>
> 4 Great God, subdue this vicious Thirst,
>   This Love to Vanity and Dust;
>   Cure the vile Fever of the Mind,
>   And feed our Souls with Joys refin'd. [CXLVI]

Our fevered passions, which are *natural* to the soul, are a mortal illness that cannot be relieved except by divine intercession as it subdues our love of worldly things and satisfies us with more suitably refined joys. As the reference to ordinary experience enhanced the physical effects of the more grotesque hymns, so the simile of the third stanza enlivens this hymn. The feverish thrashing works well, even serving to disguise the extreme asceticism that Watts is proposing. (Earthly life is described in hellish terms of unquenchable thirst and interminable torment, while the ideal is indifference to all mortal attachments.)

In hymn XLVIII, the ascetic solution is again offered, this time in spite of the seemingly good and beautiful things of this world:

> 1 How vain are all things here below.
>   How false, and yet how fair!
>   Each Pleasure hath its Poison too,
>   And every Sweet a Snare.
>
> 2 The brightest Things below the Sky
>   Give but a flattering Light;
>   We should suspect some Danger nigh
>   Where we possess Delight.
>
> 3 Our dearest Joys, and nearest Friends,
>   The Partners of our Blood,
>   How they divide our wavering Minds,
>   And leave but half for God.
>
> 4 The Fondness of a Creatures Love,
>   How strong it strikes the Sense!
>   Thither the warm Affections move,
>   Nor can we call 'em thence.
>
> 5 Dear Saviour, let thy Beauties be
>   My Souls Eternal Food;

> And Grace command my Heart away
> From all created Good.

We are unable to alienate our affections from created Good except by the Grace of God. Watts movingly recalls our seemingly virtuous pleasures and human loves only to have us condemn them all as ungodly. *Divine* delight may proceed only from contemplation of the beauties of the Savior.

If the responses written into the hymns are indeed exemplary, spiritual delight is a total emotional experience, sensibility rampant. The affected believers melt in sighs and tears; they groan or they pant and dissolve. Sometimes the goal is a quasi-erotic ecstasy, sometimes quiet withdrawal. No call to action, except to sing praises to God, ever intrudes. One may honestly question the appropriateness of the more orgiastic hymns for congregational use. (Watts himself had maintained that hymns must be restrained by the limitations of the common believer.) The emotional state of the contrite Christian is described in hymn CVI, which begins:

> O if my Soul was form'd for Woe,
>   How would I vent my Sighs!
> Repentance should like Rivers flow
>   From both my streaming Eyes.

We may recall Crashaw's excessive Weeper. While the first line accounts for the implausibility of such extremity, the image of profound distress holds.

In XXXVII Jesus transforms the pained cries, sighs, and groans of the believer into something pleasantly miserable:

> *Jesus* alone shall bear my Crys
>   Up to his Father's Throne,
> He (dearest Lord) perfumes my Sighs,
>   And sweetens every Groan. [St. 5]

The transformation suggests the ecstatic enjoyment and perfect acceptability of total woe. Sighs and groans have a spiritual place, no doubt, and we find comfort in our faith, but when the outcries are cultivated in this manner, they become ends in themselves, essential to a devotional life that depends on raw sensibility for its stimulus.

The subtle relationship between this indulgence in sensibility and Watts's asceticism is important for our grasp of both the substance and the method of his hymns. We have noted that his eighteenth-century version of asceticism was an effort to span the gulf between a distant god and depraved humankind. The possibility of traditional retreat from this world had been lost as Protestantism rejected the monastic ideal. Moreover, the suppression of passion, except for ecstatic moments, that belonged to traditional retreat, was no longer viable, and certainly it was impractical for Calvinist London burghers and their families. Watts proposed an alternative retreat from the world, into the self, where we find the God and heaven of the mind. Our feelings then become the raw material of faith, and their expression in song a useful exercise toward growth in faith. Differently formulated, our sinful state, cut off as we are from God, is the reason why we must turn inward and why we suffer so. If we were strong, which we are not by definition, we would be happy:

> Whence then should Doubts and Fears arise?
> Why trickling Sorrows drown our Eyes?
> Slowly, alas, our Mind receives
> The Comforts that our Maker gives. [LX, 5]

We are left to take what pleasure we can in our inevitable grief.

Sustained misery is not humanly possible, and Watts on occasion seems to encourage a quite comfortable religiosity. He wrote in hymn XXX:

> The Sorrows of the Mind
> Be banisht from the Place!
> Religion never was design'd
> To make our Pleasures less. [St. 2]

With brusque confidence, this hymn seems to reject the pained piety, even the otherworldliness, fostered in so many others. But if we use the glossary suggested by Watts's other hymns, the "sorrows of the Mind" are tokens of our deafness to the "comforts that our Maker gives," and the Pleasures are spiritual delights, only available to the believer who has rejected "all created Good." The appearance of brusque confidence is deceptive.

Complaisant self-satisfaction was one of many moods of Watts's age that found hymn expression, reminding us that the hymns are not a systematic exposition of humanity's relationship to God. Those hymns that reject sorrow and insecurity betray no experience of sighs and groans:

> What if we trace the Globe around,
> And search from *Britain* to *Japan,*
> There shall be no Religion found
> So Just to God, so safe for Man. [CXXXI, 2]

The verse of these hymns is stripped of the imagery and the intimacy of sensibility.

Watts's visual imagination was inspired to a far greater degree by more sentimentally appealing topics:

> Our Sorrows and our Tears we pour
> Into the Bosom of our God,
> He hears us in the mournful Hour,
> And helps us bear the heavy Load. [XLVI, 5]

In such an emblem of divine comfort, all distance is transcended by the images and the tender emotion; our life pain permits contact with God.

The hymns that treat the intimate relationship between Jesus and the believer bring together all of the qualities of Watts's work: his visual and dramatic precision, his cultivation of emotional response; everyday reference; the role-playing method of instruction; and the special nature of divine delight, Watts's goal as religious poet. His favored metaphor for the love between Jesus and the individual Christian is that of erotic passion, a comparison familiar to Watts both from the Bible and from subsequent literary tradition. It suited his purpose and perhaps even yielded shock value, although our modern discomfort with human sexuality may mislead us here.

Jesus has a "charming Name"; he is "the dear Object of our Love," who "lights our Passions to a Flame" (XVI). The "Infinite Lover" (XXI) makes my dying bed

> Feel soft as downy Pillows are,
> While on his Breast I lean my Head,
> And breathe my Life out sweetly there. [XXXI, 4]

In religious transport, the singer reports Jesus' answering love: "While *Jesus* shows his Heart is mine, / And whispers, *I am his*" (LIV, 3). Certainly our longing for "Ev'ning to undress, / That we may rest with God" insists on the singer's acceptance of the metaphor.

Before the cross, the believer is acutely self-conscious:

> Thus might I hide my blushing Face
> While his dear Cross appears,
> Dissolve my Heart in Thankfulness,
> And melt my Eyes to Tears. [IX, 5]

We are embarrassed to the point of blushing, attracted to the cross, in its "dearness." Our hearts dissolve and our eyes melt. Sensibility is repeatedly fostered by the reiteration of the dearness, sweetness, even the charm of God, Heaven, and Christ, the cross, and the wounds. A natural development of the combination of dramatic situation, everyday reference, and the cultivation of religious feeling, these hymns are also items in a long tradition of erotic symbolism, deriving from the Song of Songs.

Most accounts of Watts's hymns have taken the poet at his word that the erotic element found in the *Horae Lyricae* was removed from the *Hymns and Spiritual Songs*.[13] Perhaps its combination with ascetic otherworldliness has been misleading. Watts is always careful to advise that our mortal passions are despicable, insisting that holy passion, like holy inspiration, is a different species while at the same time he draws heavily on worldly experience as an imaginative resource. As we remarked at the beginning of this chapter, Watts's asceticism conflicts with his own poetic attachment to substantial reality. The experience of the lover of Jesus is almost too realistically represented by the experience of human lovers, regardless of the seventeenth-century precedents, and we easily forget the severe principles of restraint that Watts upheld in his hymn theory:

> 5   And if no Evening Visit's paid
>   Between my Saviour and my Soul,
>   How dull the Night! how sad the Shade!
>   How mournfully the Minutes roll!
>
> 6   This flesh of mine might learn as soon
>   To live, yet part with all my Blood;

> To breath when vital Air is gone,
> Or thrive and grow without my Food.
>
> 7 *Christ* is my Light, my Life, my Care,
> My blessed Hope, my heavenly Prize;
> Dearer than all my Passions are,
> My Limbs, my Bowels, or my Eyes.
>
> 8 The Strings that twine about my Heart,
> Tortures and Racks may tear them off;
> But they can never, never part
> With their dear hold of *Christ* my Love. [C]

The picture of a disappointed lover facing a long, lonely night in the fifth stanza is followed by a review of all the essentials of physical life. The superiority of divine love to all such physical claims is summarized in the metaphysical conceit of stanza 8, in which the heart is bound to Christ more inseparably than to the veins that feed into it. The physical details are designed to encourage overcommitment to the metaphor of divine love, just as the physical agony of the Crucifixion was intensified, forcing our response.

The divine love hymns are, in theory, made possible by the restraint of devotional purpose and the premise of ascetic denial of the flesh ("Give me new Passions, Joys and Fears, / And turn the Stone to Flesh"[CXXX]). Control of these hymns is dependent on Watts's repeated reminders that earthly passions, limbs, bowels, and eyes are of little or no importance. He appears to permit neither worldly pleasure nor self-acceptance, trying to limit the conventional analogy, forcing it to work in one direction only, bringing to life the intimacy between the believer and the Savior without sanctifying sensuality. Grotesque intrusions often serve to remind the singers of the spirituality of the experience being celebrated:

> Sprinkled afresh with pard'ning Blood
> I lay me down to rest,
> As in th' Embraces of my God,
> Or on my Saviour's Breast. [VII, 6]

The blood sprinkling colors the picture of going to bed on the breast of Jesus, embraced by God, the grotesque preliminary harnessing the image with bizarre, if spiritually edifying, results.

The survival of the analogy, regardless of the restrictions of ascetic denial and the grotesque intrusions, indicates Watts's primary allegiance, as a hymn writer, to the affective power of poetry. The potential benefit of the divine love hymns, as they worked on the imaginations of the singers, impressing them with their passionate, physical dependence on the Lord, was worth the risk to the spirit of denial. As in the preface to the *Horae Lyricae,* Watts's faith in the evangelical power of stirring poetry supersedes his own distrust of the world of sinful flesh and the tempting Fancy. Poetry wins.[14]

Watts's Achievement

We have suggested that the primary purpose of Watts's hymns, in theory and in practice, was the controlled education of the religious sensibility of his singers. The passions are rehearsed in response to affecting scenes. The visual precision of these hymns is essential to their purpose, making visible and immediate what through time or distance or distraction may have become obscured. Such visibility and immediacy—of God in heaven, Bible stories, the working of the Sacrament, the ecstasy of divine love—are intended to rouse in the singers the pious passions of love, fear, hope, desire, sorrow, wonder, and joy. These hymns called for clear, powerful poetry, finely tuned to the common psyche.

The Mark Lane setting of prosperous, educated London Independency suited Watts's talent and distinguishes his hymns from those of many of his successors. He wrote for a relatively sophisticated, homogeneous group that could be trusted to understand and to respond appropriately to his verses. His parishioners' familiarity with the Bible and with exegetical tradition, their schooling in sermons and psalms, provided a quantity of possible reference and recollection that facilitated excellent poetry. The Mark Lane flock and their fellow Independents, moreover, reliably responded as he wished to Watts's affecting stimuli, and trust was essential to the literature of sensibility. While he wrote of the limitations of the "plainer sort of Christians" and the poetic restraint necessarily exercised by the hymn writer if such people were to be properly moved, the task of reaching out to all the singers and teaching them to feel was easier in Watts's setting than it would be for Wesley or at Olney.

If Watts's method demanded his precise comprehension of and sympathy with the difficulties of these singers' spiritual lives, the hymns suggest that they, both the "politer part of Mankind" and those of "the meanest Capacity," had challenged him to make religion *matter,* by means of poetry, in the midst of their secular concerns. Both the intense, frequently jolting imagery, broken in upon by responsive sighs and groans, and the ascetic call for withdrawal from the crowd to a "sweet Retirement within our selves" indicate the need for effort to achieve spiritual experience, to "find" God. The inspirational charge laid to hymns thus far surpassed any expectations of psalms. Moreover, if Watts could, through poetry, make visible the invisible, make his singers respond to that to which they had formerly been indifferent, and clarify certain doctrinal points, he asked more of hymn poetry certainly than most of us ask of "odes."

In his defense of religious poetry, Watts had particularly stressed its efficacy, its usefulness as a means of advancing and refining devotion. Like so much didactic poetry theory, his formulations easily mislead us if we miss the respect for pure poetry that they imply. (Misled, we undervalue the hymns as poetry.) Watts was no strict utilitarian. He trusted the pleasure of poetry to uplift and to educate, to "elevate us to the most delightful and divine sensations." By being divine and, in fact, devotionally instructive, the delight was no less pure. A piety that stressed the lively feelings of the believer turned naturally to poetry. The power to move the singers' emotions in response to recognition of absolute truth belongs to pure poetry uncompromised by any ulterior motives. Within Watts's critical frame, poetry is elevated in importance rather than subordinated to utilitarian ends. Despite the formal limitations of set meters and the imaginative limitations of poetry for popular consumption, the hymns were designed to achieve all that was expected of devotional lyrics. They, no less than the more elaborate odes of the *Horae Lyricae,* ask that the poet "dress the Scenes of Religion in their proper figures of Majesty, Sweetness and Terror" in order to "diffuse Vertue and allure Souls to God." Watts encourages us to regard the hymns as a purer poetry, for all their necessary limitations. The stripping away of "flow'ry Expressions that gratify'd the Fancy" cost nothing that was ultimately to the point.

Watts's belief in the power of poetry was no simple trust. He defended the idea of religious poetry and its usefulness and wrote lyrics and hymns that are quite daring but hesitated nonetheless, restrained by a suspicion of the vagaries of the fancy and the temptations of worldliness. He both believed, or alternately believed, that humankind was salvable by means of a poetic appeal to the passions *and* that our depravity and the contamination of "all things here below" were absolute. The prospect of utter damnation, certainly, discouraged any indulgence in sensibility. The stress implicit in the very different premises of Watts's own traditional theology and his devotional aesthetics—no less his own—remained. The suspicion of profane poetry reflected in the preface to the *Horae Lyricae* balanced and controlled any tendency Watts might have had toward either overindulgence in sentiment or imaginative flights not quite to the purpose of the hymns. Watts's ambivalence was one more feature of his mind that suited his paternity of the English hymn.

Such a double allegiance is also one manifestation of the larger synthesis that underlies all of Watts's work, the attempted integration of traditional approaches to Protestant material with the new literature of the early eighteenth century. Watts's appreciation of Christian spectacle is traditional. His dramatic flair, apparent in his own mention of hymn "scenes" and in his little plays and large tableaux, recalls to mind the seventeenth-century masques, emblems, and heroic drama. In their appeal to the eye, they also resemble the German hymns of the same period. The strong images, in their substantial, forceful demonstration of religious truth, are both entertaining and memorable. Their success generally depends upon the singers' familiarity with biblical material and the conventions of devotional literature, including the traditional images of blood and wounds, worms and death, and divine love.

Watts's departure from tradition, which affected the presentation of the material, was his strong emphasis on the inwardness of religious experience, its seat in the passions. While the individual focus and introspection of Calvinist tradition had perhaps pointed the way, Watts goes further, his confidence in the ability of the passions to serve pious education suggesting the new "enlightened" trust in the native resources of humanity, in its educability. The sentimental moralists maintained that, if our better feelings are touched, we will advance in virtue, a conviction that underlies much of the poetry of

Pope and even the satires of Swift. Watts's version identifies virtue and piety: the rousing of our pious passions stimulates our "Zeal and Devotion." The general interest of the day in moral philosophy and psychology played its part, radically modifying what had been a simple sense of the accountability of each individual for his or her thoughts and deeds. Watts suggests that our spiritual sensitivity, like its moral equivalent, can be advanced and refined through exercise. His interest in the common psyche, his use of general mankind and its perceptions as a starting point in his hymns, and his commitment to the refinement of the religious sensibility are all traceable to this contemporary tendency.

The constructive tension between Watts's traditionalism and his radical modernity—for such it was in 1707—as it manifested itself both in moral theology and in poetic theory, yielded the English hymn. Tradition asked that the hymns be controlled and reasonable, that they avoid enthusiasm. Affective pious poetry asked that the singers be touched. The verse of modern poets had been considered improper for congregational use. The new age suggested that whatever penetrated the indifference of the multitudes was justifiable. The wave of the immediate future belonged to the enthusiasts, whose belief in hymns was unrestrained by Calvinist worries about either human inadequacy or original composition, and for them traditional spectacle mattered much less than sensational charismatic experience. Restraint of a different sort would appear in the Olney collection, fifty years later.

❧ III ❧

Charles Wesley:
Self, Sense, & the Revival

Conversion & Sensibility

John Wesley regarded the movement he had led as involving enlightenment of the spirit and understanding, encompassing sense and poetry, and the hymns of his brother as evangelical tools, performing the work of conversion essential to religious revival. In 1757, after twenty successful years, he could write of Methodist singing:

When it is seasonable to sing praise to GOD they do it with the spirit and with the understanding also; not in the miserable, scandalous doggerel of Hopkins and Sternhold, but in psalms and hymns which are both sense and poetry, such as would sooner dispose a critic to turn Christian than a Christian to turn critic.

John proclaimed the stylistic brilliance of Methodist song as well as its inspirational power, announcing, as Dryden never could for himself or for Shakespeare: "In these Hymns there is no doggerel, no botches, nothing put in to patch up the rhyme, no feeble expletives. Here is nothing turgid or bombast." The Methodists did not lack self-assurance.[1]

Despite John's dislike of Sternhold and Hopkins, the psalms were not forgotten. Charles paraphrased them, and more significantly, Methodist churchgoers continued to sing psalms, not hymns, in the service. As they remained worshiping Anglicans, Charles wrote his thousands of hymns for field meetings and other extraliturgical settings, a difference that tells in the design.

The excitement of the revival, the scale and importance of its evangelical campaign, were items of its faith, its success a source of joy and pride. The confident enthusiasm enlivens many of Charles Wesley's hymns:

> 1   See how great a Flame aspires,
>   Kindled by a Spark of Grace!
>   JESU's Love the Nations fires,
>   Sets the Kingdoms on a Blaze.
>   To bring Fire on Earth he came;
>   Kindled in some Hearts it is;
>   O that All might catch the Flame,
>   All partake the glorious Bliss!
>
> 2   When He first the Work begun,
>   Small and feeble was his Day;
>   Now the Word doth swiftly run,
>   Now it wins its widening Way,
>   More and more it spreads, and grows,
>   Ever mighty to prevail,
>   Sin's strong-holds it now o'erthrows,
>   Shakes the trembling Gates of Hell.[2]

The success of the revival is seen as a spreading fire, a swift military takeover, a sky quickly filling with rain clouds. The mood is one of confidence and accomplishment.

The personal drama of charismatic conversion lay behind the public drama of mass revival and the confidence and enthusiasm in and for the cause. In the conversion pattern, private despair was understood as efficacious as it led to the moment of enlightenment. The conversion experience resolved all conflicts and yielded a joyful quietude. For purpose of contrast and emphasis, each of these stages referred to the others in hymn representation. Hymn XVII was written to celebrate the anniversary of Wesley's own conversion. After 1740 the first six stanzas were eliminated from hymnals, perhaps because they were considered too personal for general use. It is precisely these stanzas, however, that illustrate the personal drama at the heart of the Methodist experience, verses that Charles, when he wrote them, felt suitable for a congregational hymn:

> 1   Glory to GOD, and Praise, and Love
>   Be ever, ever given;
>   By Saints below, and Saints above,
>   The Church in Earth and Heaven.

2   On this glad Day the glorious Sun
        Of Righteousness arose,
    On my benighted Soul he shone,
        And fill'd it with Repose.

3   Sudden expir'd the legal Strife,
        'Twas then I ceas'd to grieve,
    My Second, Real, Living Life
        I then began to live.

4   Then with my *Heart* I first believ'd,
        Believ'd, with Faith Divine,
    Power with the Holy Ghost receiv'd
        To call the Saviour *Mine*.

5   I felt my LORD's Atoning Blood
        Close to *my* Soul applied;
    Me, me he lov'd—the Son of GOD
        For *me,* for *me* He died!

6   I found, and own'd his Promise true,
        Ascertain'd of *my* Part,
    My Pardon pass'd in Heaven I *knew*
        When written on my Heart.

7   O for a Thousand Tongues to sing
        My dear Redeemer's Praise!
    The Glories of my GOD and King,
        The Triumphs of his Grace.

The suffering before conversion is suggested by the benighted situation of the soul and the grief that ceases at the event (stanza 2). Then the doctrinal accomplishment of conversion is explained in orthodox Protestant terms as the triumph of Grace over the legal strife of the old law. The striking quality of the hymn is most apparent, however, in stanzas 4 through 6, in which the impact of conversion on the ego is explained. "I," "me," and "mine" appear fifteen times in these three stanzas. The self is the focus and the self is assured. Given the public, didactic working of hymns, we can only conclude that this self-centering of religious experience is approved. An unconfident singer learns by example the joys of salvation, while a happy convert is reminded of his or her joyful certainty.[3]

The message of Methodism was distinct from that of the Calvinists in several vital respects, affecting both the content and the poetry of Wesley's hymns. Most obviously, the Wesleys rejected the doctrine of predestination in favor of the belief in the universal availability of salvation:

> 10 Who underfoot their Saviour trod,
>   Expos'd *afresh* and *crucified*,
> Who trampled on the SON of GOD,
>   For Them, for Them, their Saviour died.
>
> 11 For those who at the Judgment Day
>   *On Him they pierc'd* shall *look* with Pain;
> The Lamb for every *Castaway*,
>   For *Every Soul of Man* was slain.
>
> 12 Why then, Thou Universal Love,
>   Should any of thy Grace despair?
> To All, to All, Thy Bowels move,
>   But straitned in our own We are. [XX]

Such high confidence relieved the suspense over election that had resulted in the anxious tension of so many of Watts's hymns. Salvation had become rather less worrisome; damnation did not present a substantial threat.

We noted in the last chapter that another, related source of strain was the contrast between a distant, indifferent God and depraved humankind incapable of self-improvement beyond an inevitably futile effort at ascetic removal from mundane affairs. Once again, the Wesleys bring relief. God is neither threatening nor distant, and his mortals have little trouble improving upon their situation. The kindliness and concern of Jesus are particularly prominent. In hymn XXIII, based on Psalm 51:10, Jesus becomes a proper "man of feeling," a compassionate type who was, in much contemporary literature, the only man of virtue:

> Thy tender Heart is still the same,
>   And melts at Human Woe:
> JESU, for Thee distrest I am,
>   I want Thy Love to know. [St. 5]

The Miltonic standard is useful for the purpose of distinguishing the particularly eighteenth-century features of Wesley's hymns. Milton's Son of God pitied humanity certainly, but his tender heart did not melt. Milton was not "distressed" for Jesus. The incarnation is presented in other hymns (XXXVIII, XLI) as the manifestation of God's friendliness. Elsewhere God is particularly the friend of sinners.

Charismatic conversion experience, guaranteed salvation, and a sense of intimacy between God and humanity resolved the tension that had inspired Watts to call on the powerful resources of bloody violence and divine love. In this different context, in which the Calvinist strain had been relieved, these conventions were no longer needed. Accordingly, the use of spectacle for dramatic impact is different in Wesley's hymns. The responses of the singers are enthusiastic items in the new tradition of the cult of feeling, demonstrated by the broken speech patterns. This different understanding of the essence of religious experience, taken in combination with the revival setting, which begged a different didactic approach, results in the characteristic Wesleyan hymn.[4]

In Charles's hymns, the theatrical and dramatic display, which is one means used to meet the obligation of hymns to "entertain" their singers, is not the neat, cohesive presentation found in Watts's work. Description is always subordinated to its subjective significance, and logical continuity is frequently sacrificed. Perhaps the size and variety of Wesley's audience, so unlike Watts's Independent congregations, demanded a more heavy-handed devotional discipline, even to the extent of mistrusting the singers' spontaneous reactions to religious tableaux. But beyond this difference in circumstances, the desirability of intense religious feelings is the true subject of a great number of hymns. Feelings are instrumental in both the provocation of and the reaction to one's personal salvation. In terms of our theatrical analogy, we find that the devout singer-spectator of Watts's tableaux has become an active participant in Wesleyan hymn drama. In the "Hymn of Thanksgiving to the Father" (II), the story of the prodigal son is dramatized, with the individual singer playing the role of the son:

> 1   Thee, O my GOD and King,
>   My Father, Thee I sing!
>   Hear well-pleas'd the joyous Sound,
>   Praise from Earth and Heav'n receive;

Lost, I now in CHRIST am found,
    Dead, by Faith in CHRIST I live.

2   Father, behold thy Son,
            In CHRIST I am thy own.
    Stranger long to Thee and Rest,
        See the Prodigal is come:
    Open wide thine Arms and Breast,
        Take the weary Wand'rer home.

3   Thine Eye observ'd from far,
            Thy Pity look'd me near:
    Me thy Bowels yearn'd to see,
        Me thy Mercy ran to find,
    Empty, poor, and void of Thee,
        Hungry, sick, and faint, and blind.

4   Thou on my Neck didst fall,
            Thy Kiss forgave me all:
    Still the gracious Words I hear,
        Words that made the Saviour mine,
    Haste, for Him the Robe prepare,
        His be Righteousness Divine!

5   Thee then, my GOD and King,
            My Father, Thee I sing!
    Hear well-pleas'd the joyous Sound,
        Praise from Earth and Heav'n receive;
    Lost, I now in CHRIST am found,
        Dead, by Faith in CHRIST I live.

The experience of the prodigal son is acted out in such a fashion that the participatory identification of the singer with the son is inescapable. This identification determines the address of the hymn to God the compassionate father. However, a drama on the prodigal son theme for the benefit of God is relatively pointless, so Wesley has designed the testimony of the son-singer both for the benefit of the singer's own understanding and to share the good news with the unconverted.[5] The result of this complex of aims is a disjointed narrative that shifts its address frequently. A further source of confusion is the alternation of tenses in this hymn. The tense of the first two stanzas, a dramatic present, jars with the past tense of the subsequent stanzas, recalling the moment of supreme acceptance and the preliminary misery.

The involvement of the singers in the activity of the hymns often upsets their neat presentation. In hymn LIV, a tableau of the Crucifixion is repeatedly interrupted by exclamation, injunction, interpretation, and response. The precision of Watts's vision is missing:

> 2   Endless Scenes of Wonder rise
>   With that mysterious Tree,
>   Crucified before our Eyes
>   Where we our Maker see:
>   JESUS, LORD, what hast Thou done!
>   Publish we the Death Divine,
>   Stop, and gaze, and fall, and own
>   Was never Love like Thine!
>
> 3   Never Love nor Sorrow was
>   Like that my JESUS show'd;
>   See Him stretch'd on yonder Cross
>   And crush'd beneath our Load!
>   Now discern the Deity,
>   Now his heavenly Birth declare!
>   Faith cries out 'Tis He, 'tis He,
>   My GOD that suffers there!

The descriptive promise of the second stanza is disrupted by the exclamation directed at Jesus, then the evangelical call to publish the news, followed by the prescribed amazement, and finally, once again addressed to Jesus, an exclamation about his love. The syntactical confusion even suggests in the last two lines of the second stanza that Jesus is to stop and gaze and fall.

In the third stanza, the injunction to see is not the same indicator, familiar from the hymns of Watts, that a scene has been painted before our eyes. The elements do not coalesce but are rather lost in a rush of response. In their urgency, the references tumble in:

> 4   JESUS drinks the bitter Cup;
>   The Wine-press treads alone,
>   Tears the Graves and Mountains up
>   By his expiring Groan:
>   Lo! the Powers of Heaven He shakes;

> Nature in Convulsions lies,
> Earth's profoundest Centre quakes,
> The great *Jehovah* dies!

Our metaphorical eyes cannot focus on such a simultaneous drinking, treading, tearing up, expiring groaning, and shaking. The hymn culminates in an expression of the broken heart of the singer:

> 7 O my GOD, he dies for me,
>   I feel the mortal Smart!
> See Him hanging on the Tree—
>   A Sight that breaks my Heart!
> O that all to Thee might turn!
>   Sinners ye may love him too,
> Look on Him ye pierc'd and mourn
>   For One who bled for You.

That the histrionic sympathy of the singer is more important than the precise vision of the cross for Wesley's purpose is seen in the turn of the last two lines, in which the devastated response is recommended to sinners in yet another shift of address. (The first two lines are introspective, the second two lines seem addressed to a fellow believer, the fifth addresses Christ, and the last three call to the wider world of sinners.)

If the larger visual picture is rarely developed, Wesley often employed theatrical effects to serve his ends. In hymn LVII the atonement works in almost cinematic fashion:

> 3 The Smoke of thy Atonement here
>   Darken'd the Sun and rent the Vail,
> Made the New Way to Heaven appear,
>   And shew'd the great Invisible:
> Well pleas'd in Thee our GOD look'd down,
> And call'd his Rebels to a Crown.

> 4 He still respects thy Sacrifice,
>   It's Savour Sweet doth always please,
> The Offering smoaks thro' Earth and Skies,
>   Diffusing Life and Joy and Peace,
> To thee thy lower Courts it comes,
> And fills them with Divine Perfumes.

The two stanzas are unified in address and by the odor and effect of the offering. Only mild confusion proceeds from the address to Jesus of a hymn that explains the atonement for the benefit of the singers, suggesting that the explanation is intended for the Lord.

Hymn XCII anticipates the coming of the Kingdom. Theatrical machinery and a cast of thousands make of this hymn something of a biblical spectacular:

> 1 Lo! He comes with clouds descending,
>   Once for favour'd sinners slain!
> Thousand, thousand saints attending,
>   Swell the triumph of his train:
>   Hallelujah,
>   GOD appears, on earth to reign!
>
> 2 Every eye shall now behold Him
>   Rob'd in dreadful majesty,
> Those who set at nought and sold Him,
>   Pierc'd, and nail'd Him to the tree,
>   Deeply wailing
> Shall the true Messiah see.
>
> 3 The dear tokens of his passion
>   Still his dazling body bears,
> Cause of endless exultation
>   To his ransom'd worshippers;
>   With what rapture
> Gaze we on those glorious scars!
>
> 4 Yea, amen! let all adore Thee
>   High on thine eternal throne
> Saviour, take the power and glory
>   Claim the kingdom for thine own:
>   JAH, JEHOVAH,
>   Everlasting GOD, come down.

In the first stanza the singers, as a group, are transformed into saints, attending the descent of Christ at the last day. In the second stanza the singers withdraw from the scene to observe the effect of the Coming on the betrayers of Christ. We have entered the future. The clarity of the vision dissolves with the syntax as, by stanza 3, the dearness of the tokens and the gratitude and rapture of the singers have become the focal point of the hymn. The noise of exultation seems incompatible with the dazzling glory and the presumable silence of gazing and rapture. The last stanza cancels the picture of the preceding three as we return to the present and Jesus returns to his heavenly throne.

The shifting address is often difficult to follow. Hymn LXXXVII is a reflection on the experience of Thomas:

> 4   Breathe on us, LORD, in this our Day,
>   And these dry Bones shall live,
>   Speak Peace into our Hearts, and say
>   The HOLY GHOST receive.
>
> 5   Whom now we seek O might we meet!
>   JESUS the Crucified,
>   Shew us thy bleeding Hands and Feet,
>   Thou who for us hast died.
>
> 6   Cause us thy Record to receive,
>   Speak, and the Tokens shew,
>   "O be not faithless, but believe
>   In me, who died for You."
>
> 7   LORD, I believe for me, ev'n me
>   Thy Wounds were open'd wide,
>   I see the Prints, I more than see
>   Thy Feet, thy Hands, thy Side.
>
> 8   I cannot fear, I cannot doubt,
>   I feel the sprinkled Blood:
>   Let every Soul with me cry out
>   Thou art my LORD, my GOD!

The first stanza reproduced above is addressed to Jesus by the group. The next stanza begins with a collective wishful sigh, addressed to nobody in particular. Jesus is then asked for the signs of redemption, as the singers play the part of Thomas. The commitment to the role is imperfect, however, as the identity of Jesus is affirmed. Then, in direct discourse, Jesus speaks to the singer. In stanza 7, the first person singular is substituted for the plural as the individual singer addresses his believing response to Jesus. In the eighth stanza, the self addresses itself, then turns to the other believers, asking that they say, finally, to Jesus, "Thou art my LORD, my GOD!"[6]

In our survey of Watts's hymns, we found that the descriptive clarity and dramatic integrity often forced the singers to visualize scenes of bloody streams and bowing worms. Wesley also employs these images, but a different effect is obtained because they are subordinated to his larger purpose, a purpose quite distinct from that of Watts. We do not dwell on the blood:

> 7 Come O my guilty Brethren come,
>   Groaning beneath your Load of Sin!
>   His bleeding Heart shall make you room,
>   His open Side shall take you in.
>   He calls you Now, invites you home—
>   Come, O my guilty Brethren, come!
>
> 8 For you the purple Current flow'd
>   In Pardons from his wounded Side:
>   Languish'd for you th'Eternal GOD,
>   For you the Prince of Glory dy'd.
>   *Believe:* and all your Guilt's forgiven,
>   *Only Believe*—and yours is Heaven. [I]

Our entry into the bleeding heart and opened side of Jesus, issuing a purple current, ought to be a sensational picture of the Watts type, but it is not. We may suggest several reasons for the difference. First of all, the image is unrelated to common experience. In his blood-and-wounds hymns, Watts had referred to daily habits of eating and drinking. Wesley's entry into the pleura is not so immediate. Secondly, the assurance of salvation that motivates the invitation has relieved the tension that Watts cultivated. Force is no longer required, nor is the violent image necessary. Thirdly, the revivalist voice of the hymn, in its loud confidence, is addressed to the crowd, to "you." The emphasis is on the call to faith, not on the bleeding and groaning of the crucified Son of God. The vision is no longer stark and terrible; it is surrounded by an appreciative crowd. Finally, the multiplicity of incompatible images of these stanzas undermines the dramatic impact of the scene. The spectacle of a crowd of people, carrying large bundles of sin, is effective—until we are asked to visualize their entry into the bleeding heart, which is actively hosting them, then calling them, inviting them home. We cannot tell precisely what is happening.

In hymn XXIX we have another example of the Wesleyan use of blood and wounds:

1   Arise, my Soul, arise,
         Shake off thy guilty Fears,
      The Bleeding Sacrifice
         In my Behalf appears;
    Before the Throne my Surety stands;
    My Name is written on His Hands.

2   He ever lives above
         For me to interceed,
      His All-redeeming Love,
         His pretious Blood to plead;
    His Blood aton'd for All our Race,
    And sprinkles now the Throne of Grace.

3   Five bleeding Wounds He bears,
         Receiv'd on *Calvary;*
      They pour effectual Prayers,
         They strongly speak for me;
    Forgive him, O forgive, they cry,
    Nor let that Ransom'd Sinner die!

Each of these three stanzas is replete with bloody reference: the ghostly apparition of the bleeding sacrifice, the blood-sprinkled throne, the wounds pouring blood. Nevertheless, the assurance of salvation preempts all horror as all the images are carefully linked to the individual saved soul. They are evidence of salvation rather than objects of enforced contemplation. From the Calvinist-Pietist viewpoint of Watts, depraved humanity confronted a devastatingly violent torture on Calvary. Wesley's singers can cope with the bleeding sacrifice because they are certain that it is all for their benefit. In the first stanza alone, precisely those guilty fears that inspired Watts's devotion are seen as incompatible with faith. Once again, the different use of blood and horror is reflected in Wesley's compounded imagery, the five wounds that not only bleed but also cry out in prayer for the singers.[7]

A second salient feature of Watts's hymns was his employment of a sexual model for the love between man and God. We found this to be one result of a combination of Pietistic otherworldliness and a need to comprehend some form of intimacy between God, who seemed distant, and man in his sin. Neither motive inspired Wesley, and divine love is undeveloped in his hymns. John Wesley did deny a place in the Methodist canon to one of his brother's hymns, perhaps suspecting it of such imagery. "JESU, Lover of my Soul" (XV) is a very moderate illustration of the type:

1   JESU, Lover of my Soul,
         Let me to Thy Bosom fly,
     While the nearer Waters roll,
         While the Tempest still is high:
     Hide me, O my Saviour, hide,
         Till the Storm of Life is past:
     Safe into the Haven guide;
         O receive my Soul at last.

2   Other Refuge have I none,
         Hangs my helpless Soul on Thee:
     Leave, ah! leave me not alone,
         Still support, and comfort me.
     All my Trust on Thee is stay'd;
         All my Help from Thee I bring;
     Cover my defenceless Head,
         With the Shadow of thy Wing.

3   Wilt Thou not regard my Call?
         Wilt Thou not accept my Prayer?
     Lo! I sink, I faint, I fall—
         Lo! on Thee I cast my Care:
     Reach me out Thy gracious Hand!
         While I of Thy Strength receive,
     Hoping against Hope I stand,
         Dying, and behold I live!

Despite the title line, we receive the impression, not of a lover-God, but rather of God as refuge, into whose bosom one retreats from the storm of life. The mood is that of intense desperation rather than languor. In the spirit of desperation, the metaphors tumble in, one on top of another, until it is difficult to trace the action of the hymn. Jesus is the lover who hides the singer from rough weather while at the same time the singer hangs on Jesus and worries about his leaving. Jesus then shadows the singer with his *wing*. In the third stanza the prospect of rejected prayer provokes a breakdown. A spirit of hope and trust is gradually built up in the following two stanzas:

4   Thou, O CHRIST, art all I want,
         More than all in Thee I find:

> Raise the Fallen, chear the Faint,
>   Heal the Sick, and lead the Blind,
> Just, and Holy is Thy Name,
>   I am all unrighteousness,
> False, and full of Sin I am,
>   Thou art full of Truth, and Grace.
>
> 5 Plenteous Grace with Thee is found,
>   Grace to cover all my Sin:
>   Let the healing Streams abound,
>   Make, and keep me pure within:
>   Thou of Life the Fountain art:
>   Freely let me take of Thee,
>   Spring Thou up within my Heart,
>   Rise to all Eternity!

Charles had gone too far, not in imaging forth divine love, but in his chaotic accumulation of imagery and loss of devotional focus. In stanza 4, we begin with an acclamation of Christ's sufficiency, proceed to a brusque prayer for the raising, cheering, healing, and leading of mortals, then read a statement of the contrast between divine righteousness and human sin. In the following stanza, abundance, healing streams, and purification are followed by images of the fountain of life, the singer's heart, and resurrection. No relationship is established among these many ideas.

Feeling & the Exemplary Method

One might be tempted to dismiss the less coherent hymns of Wesley as poetic failures, excused by the famous horseback composition, or as inevitable lapses in an oeuvre of 9,000 items. One might further suggest that the splendid new music hid a multitude of failings, or that Wesley's singers, compared with Watts's parishioners, were uncritical. We would rather propose that Wesley knew precisely what he was doing and that his hymns cultivated enthusiastic response, the kind of emotional intensity that led to conversion and then lived on with reference to it. This cult of feeling is unrestrained by Watts's traditional, contemplative Pietism. The shifting address and plethora of reference and observation are calculated means to the desired ends, purposes revealed in another fashion in the more coherent hymns.

The rush of illustration and metaphor intensifies devotional sorrow, transforming it into desperation; the structural failure in the more joyful hymns builds the joy into ecstasy. Charismatic religious experience sprang from just such cultivated despair and yielded just such ecstatic moments. The responses written into the hymns indicate that Wesley's manipulation of his singers' feelings was deliberate, controlled, and directed by this kind of evangelical purpose.

The cultivation of feeling is at odds with otherworldliness, a contradiction implicit in the hymns of Watts but not felt in Wesley's. For Wesley, the world is not particularly contaminated. The pains of life are useful spurs to faith and worldly joys a genuine comfort, only to be rejected as they keep us from efficacious suffering:

> 4   All Earthly Comforts I disdain,
>   They shall not rob me of my Pain,
>   Or make me senseless of my Load,
>   Or less disconsolate for GOD.
>
> 5   Rather let all the Creatures take
>   Their Miserable Comforts back,
>   With every vain Relief depart,
>   And leave me to my Broken Heart. [XXVIII]

Our pain is a precious possession, and our broken hearts are preferable to relief.

In hymn XIV, interpreting the Beatitudes in this new light, the salvation of the Christian man or woman of feeling is guaranteed by Christ:

> 2   Thou hast pronounced the Mourner blest,
>   And Lo! for Thee I ever mourn:
>   I cannot; no! I will not rest,
>   Till Thou my only Rest return,
>   Till Thou, the Prince of Peace, appear,
>   And I receive the Comforter.

We *will* our grief. Incessant longing is a means of grace, to be nurtured within. The desired suffering, in its immediacy, breaks into the speech pattern of the hymn, reflecting the language of strong feeling ("I cannot; no! I will not rest"). In the following stanza, the singers lay similar claim to the blessing accorded those who hunger and thirst after righteousness:

> 3 Where is the Blessedness bestow'd
>   On all that hunger after Thee?
>   I hunger now, I thirst for GOD!
>   See, the poor, fainting Sinner see,
>   And satisfy with endless Peace,
>   And fill me with Thy Righteousness.

The lesson the singers are to learn is that they will be blessed if they display their longing to the eye of God. It is even implied that God is obligated by some contract to meet the terms of his promise, with no questions asked abut the unusual nature of their hunger.

Strong feeling is desirable as a means of grace. It is the substance of prayer as well. Our feelings reveal God and are in direct communication with him:

> 4 Ah LORD!—if Thou art in that Sigh,
>   Then hear Thyself within me pray.
>   Hear in my Heart Thy Spirit's Cry,
>   Mark what my lab'ring Soul *would* say,
>   Answer the deep, unutter'd Groan,
>   And shew that Thou and I are One.

We, and God, can hear the voice of the spirit by attending to our sighing and inner groaning.

Longing and languishing after God were rewarded with the raptures of mystical consummation, in which the singers were to be relieved of all this straining. The ecstatic end was perfectly passive:

> 1   O Mercy Divine
>   How couldst Thou incline
>   My GOD to become such an Infant as *mine!*
>
> . . . .
>
> 14   Like him would I be,
>   My Master I see
>   In a Stable; a Stable shall satisfy me.

15   With Him I reside:
          The Manger shall hide
      Mine Honour: the Manger shall bury my Pride.

16   And here will I lie,
          Till rais'd up on high
      With Him on the Cross I recover the Sky. [L]

The Christian is called to join the infant in the manger, almost literally. It is suggested that the meaning of the Incarnation is that we are to revert to the helplessness and inactivity of infancy for the duration of this life.

The movement toward mystical consummation was both natural and tortuous. Frantic longing characterized the waiting period, but at the same time Wesley could not quite say that the longing earned the believer his or her salvation, as that would not conform to the Protestant belief in the justification by grace alone. He regularly stopped short of such a cause-and-effect understanding of the relationship between longing and reward:

> Ever upward let us move,
> Wafted on the Wings of Love,
> Looking when our LORD shall come,
> Longing, gasping after Home. [X, 9]

The passive conveyance on the wings of Love is inconsistent with the second couplet, which suggests passionate discomfort. Since the hymns were meant to train the singers in appropriate religious response, these two moods, longing and glassy surrender, must be considered exemplary.

As the manger was interpreted as a model for passive surrender, so the followers of the shepherd were drawn to the quiet immobility of sheep at rest:

1   Thou Shepherd of *Israel,* and mine,
          The joy and desire of my heart,
     For closer communion I pine,
          I long to reside where thou art;
     The pasture I languish to find
          Where all who their Shepherd obey,

> Are fed, on thy bosom reclin'd,
>   Are skreen'd from the heat of the day.

The pining, longing, and languishing take as their object a heaven in which the desired communion is the exceedingly passive condition of being fed while lying in the shade. In the second stanza, the joy of heaven is frozen in an icy tableau:

> 2 Ah, shew me that happiest place,
>   That place of thy people's abode,
>   Where saints in an extasy gaze,
>   And hang on a crucified GOD:
>   Thy love for a sinner declare,
>   Thy passion and death on the tree,
>   My spirit to *Calvary* bear,
>   To suffer, and triumph, with thee.

All the activity belongs to God. Even the saints can only gaze in ecstasy, hang on Jesus, or be borne in spirit to the cross. In a typical shift in vision, the following stanza clusters the sheep of the first around the cross, become rock, then raises them to hide in the open side of Christ:

> 3 'Tis there with the lambs of thy flock,
>   There only I covet to rest,
>   To lie at the foot of the Rock,
>   Or rise to be hid in thy breast;
>   'Tis there I would always abide,
>   And never a moment depart,
>   Conceal'd in the clift of thy side,
>   Eternally held in thy heart. [CI]

To rest, to lie, to hide, to abide concealed, eternally held: even on Calvary, one rests, rising only to be hidden. Martha England has written of Charles Wesley's hymns, "Verbs are active, imperative, urgent. Talk, see, strike, lift, teach, look, receive, come."[8] We note, however, that the truly active verbs in this list have God as subject. Humanity is instructed in pining.

In Wesley's adaptation of Psalm 125 the relationship between our desire and mystical consummation is suggested, refining the contrast between tortured longing and passive obliteration:

> Turn us again, O Lord,
> Pronounce the second Word,
> Loose our Hearts, and let us go
> Down the Spirit's fullest Flood,
> Freely to the Fountain flow,
> All be swallow'd up in God. [XXXI, 5]

The flood of our own spiritual feeling is to carry us to a fountain that swallows us up, obliterating the self. Our feelings are our means of spiritual locomotion. They naturally flow toward God, and the journey is rewarded by the desired annihilation of the self. The unavoidable suggestion is the natural goodness of human feeling, in Shaftesbury's sense. Only our feelings have an active role to play in the spiritual drive toward consummation.

Charles Wesley could stress either pining or ecstatic passivity or could combine the two in a given hymn. In "Rapturous Height" (LXXIII), recalling an ecstatic "high," the pleasures of that moment are described in free-swinging anapests:

> 5   On the Wings of his Love
>   I was carried above
> All Sin, and Temptation, and Pain;
>   I could not believe
>   That I ever should grieve,
> That I ever should suffer again.
>
> 6   I rode on the Sky
>   (Freely justified I!)
> Nor envied *Elijah* his Seat;
>   My Soul mounted higher
>   In a Chariot of Fire,
> And the Moon it was under my Feet.
>
> 7   O the rapturous Height
>   Of that holy Delight,
> Which I felt in the Life-giving Blood!
>   Of my Saviour possest,
>   I was perfectly blest,
> As if fill'd with the Fulness of GOD.

This hymn, without the more personal stanzas, including 5 and 6, repeatedly found a place in the Methodist hymnals. Recollection of free-riding rapture must have reminded the singers of the joys they had known or of the joys in store. Spiritual sensation is the substance of the hymn, obviously a source of great pleasure.

The vital importance of individual emotional experience indicates that the preeminent characteristic of Wesley's hymns is their subjectivity, when subjectivity is understood as qualified by the requirements of the congregational hymn. The singers' feelings are encouraged and directed in response to each hymn subject. They self-consciously inject themselves into Bible stories, becoming actors in hymn-drama. They read their names on the Lord's hands. They pine and gaze together. They are directed to relate the subject matter of faith to their own emotions. Emotion is assigned a positive value, to the extent of dissolving hymn logic in feeling display. This appreciation of religious emotion is a very distant relative of the highly controlled sensibility and careful use of visual stimuli found in Watts's hymns.

Certainly we would misunderstand Wesleyan subjectivity if we read the hymns as straightforward personal confession, which would be unsuitable for congregational song. Ernest Rattenbury was troubled by the relationship between the poet and the feelings of the hymns: "How far can Wesley's hymns be regarded as records of his own personal experience? Were they not written, as hymns usually are, for other people to sing? Did this man speak of himself or of another? Can they even be properly called hymns if they are merely confessional literature?"[9] Rattenbury devised a theory of "personation" to explain the relationship, writing that Charles was acting the parts of different believers in various circumstances, voicing their probable feelings, even somehow exorcising them. Our alternative explanation rejects personation as insufficiently edifying. Wesley's purpose was not the expressive *venting* of feeling but rather the evangelical *directing* of feeling. Emotion, roused and controlled, would carry the singer to God. Passion was a means to a didactic end, and its expression was usually exemplary.[10]

One implication of this interpretation of the emotional content of the hymns is that we cannot take the passions expressed in the hymns as a record of common feeling. They are rather expressions of how we ought to learn to feel. Because he saw the hymns as expressive, Rattenbury allowed himself to be convinced that the Methodists were genuinely joyful when their friends died: "The fact that the funeral

hymns were often written in joyous anapestic verse, apparently not
very suitable on sad occasions, expresses the triumphant joy over
death which his people felt."[11] We would suggest that the joy is
exemplary, not expressive-realistic, and the substance of a lesson the
singers were to learn.

Hymn LXIV, "On the Corpse of a Believer," illustrates the
exemplary method, showing as well its incompatibility with any
traditional contemplation of the gruesomeness of death:

> 1 Ah! lovely Appearance of Death!
>   No Sight upon Earth is so fair:
>   Not all the gay Pageants that breathe
>   Can with a dead Body compare.
>   With solemn Delight I survey
>   The Corpse, when the Spirit is fled,
>   In love with the beautiful Clay,
>   And longing to lie in its stead.
>
> 2 How blest is our Brother, bereft
>   Of all that could burthen his Mind!
>   How easy the Soul, that hath left
>   This wearisom Body behind!
>   Of Evil incapable thou,
>   Whose Relicks with Envy I see;
>   No longer in Misery now,
>   No longer a Sinner like me.
>
> 3 This Earth is affected no more
>   With Sickness, or shaken with Pain:
>   The War in the Members is o'er,
>   And never shall vex him again:
>   No Anger hence forward, or Shame,
>   Shall redden this Innocent Clay;
>   Extinct is the Animal Flame,
>   And Passion is vanish'd away.
>
> 4 This languishing Head is at rest,
>   Its Thinking and Aching are o'er;
>   This quiet immoveable Breast
>   Is heav'd by Affliction no more:
>   This Heart is no longer the Seat
>   Of Trouble and torturing Pain,

> It ceases to flutter and beat,
>   It never shall flutter again.
>
> 5   The Lids he so seldom could close,
>   By Sorrow forbidden to sleep,
>   Seal'd up in eternal Repose,
>   Have strangely forgotten to weep:
>   The Fountains can yield no Supplies,
>   These Hollows from Water are free,
>   The Tears are all wip'd from these Eyes,
>   And Evil they never shall see.
>
> 6   To mourn and to suffer is mine,
>   While bound in a Prison I breathe,
>   And still for Deliverance pine,
>   And press to the Issues of Death:
>   What now with my Tears I bedew,
>   O might I this Moment become,
>   My Spirit created anew,
>   My Flesh be consign'd to the Tomb!

This envious appreciation of the corpse of a believer is an outrageous version of the accepted belief in the resurrection of the faithful. It is untrue that dead bodies are lovely, prettier than anything else. No normal individual, however pious, is truly envious of a corpse. After challenging us with this seeming absurdity, Wesley explains himself in stanzas 2 through 4. He is preaching through his hymn, forcing the mourners to voice Christian teaching concerning the Resurrection. He does this by expressing impossible sentiments, by doing intentional violence to normal human feelings in his forceful indoctrination. Watts would have felt obliged to express a tension between life fear and death fear, beginning his hymn with common sentiments and exploiting the grimly physical potential of a deathbed hymn. Wesley has swept all common feelings aside. His aim was to force the singers to alter their most basic instincts about the sadness and repulsiveness of death. His didactic assurance is incompatible with spiritual tension of any kind. Certainly this hymn is didactic-exemplary rather than expressive-realistic.

A second illustration of the rejection of realism and simple expression is hymn XIX, teaching close Christian fellowship, which was as much a part of Methodist tradition as was field preaching. The mutual sensibility that ideally characterized the relations between humanity and our kindly God, was extended to interhuman communion:

> Sweetly now we all agree,
> Touch'd with softest Simpathy,
> Kindly for each other care:
> Every Member feels its Share:
> Wounded by the Grief of One,
> All the suffering Members groan;
> Honour'd if one Member is
> All partake the common Bliss. [St. 4]

The perfect harmony celebrated here was desirable, ideal, exemplary. Presumably the singers could master the ideal by expressing it, by learning the lines. (The hymn would be particularly meaningful in the aftermath of unpleasant conflict within the community.) We cannot conclude that the community of believers that sang this hymn was without sin.[12]

John Wesley endorsed the educational value of hymns in his preface to the 1780 collection: "The Hymns are not carelessly jumbled together, but carefully ranged under proper heads, according to the experience of real christians. So that this book is in effect a little body of experimental and practical divinity" (p. iv). While his brother Charles had indeed written edifying hymns, they are hardly versified doctrine. The subtle relationship between the singers' real life experience and the transformed perception of the convert—as the Wesleys desired that it be expressed—is as important as the doctrinal content of hymns on conversion or the universal availability of salvation.

John's defense of the Methodist hymns was needed. They were not universally recognized as lucid explication of "divinity." Indeed, contemporary critics were all too apt to find fault. One John Scott, for example, objected on numerous counts:

The Hymns they sing, i.e. all I have seen or heard of, are not rational Compositions, nor do they accord with the first Principles of all Religion, but like their Prayers, dwell upon a Word, or are immediate addresses to the Son of God, as the supreme Object of Worship. And do represent him as much more friendly and compassionate to the human World than God the Father ever was—so that their Singing is calculated to engage the Passions by nothing more than Words, and the Melody of the Sound, or Voice; but if you would sing with the Understanding, you must have other sorts of Compositions both for Psalmody and Prayer, than what the Foundery or the Tabernacle do afford you.[13]

All hymns are doctrinal, implicitly or explicitly and even by omission. At issue is the poetic handling of a dogmatic orientation. Wesley's hymns distinguish themselves by their intentional provocation of emotional response—as such they "are not rational Compositions." The composition was, however, controlled and edited by reason and was informed by Wesley's particular purpose. Scott's objections are theological (to the address to Jesus as friend, in particular) and devotional (to the calculated engagement of the passions). The suitability of hymns as Wesley wrote them to Methodism is affirmed by negatives.

The educational purpose of the Wesleyan movement is apparent as well in the role-playing hymns, in which the singer identifies with the prodigal, the baby in the manger, or Peter. While this kind of entertainment helped the singers to remember the Bible stories and their lessons, it wreaked havoc with the logical, stanza-by-stanza development of the verses as shifts of address follow the stage directions. Closely related to such role-playing is the sentimental pedagogy of the exemplary hymns, in which the singers are instructed in proper Christian feelings about the death of a friend, the Passion, the manger, or Christian fellowship. The prominent place of response and its highly strung emotional nature, while always theologically appropriate, often overwhelms the hymn as coherent poetry. We can read the doctrinal implications in the breakdown of the language.

Hymns for Preachers

The hymns that Charles Wesley wrote especially for the Methodist preachers may usefully be compared and contrasted with those intended for general use. The former are not really congregational hymns at all. In their different purpose and special application they confirm our observations about the design and method of the regular hymns. The zealous activity of the persona of these preachers' hymns suggests the excitement of the revival from the perspective of its heroes, the men and women who answered the evangelistic call.

Wesley obviously expected more of these individuals, in terms of both theological sophistication and devotional experience, than of the masses they addressed. The roles they had to learn to play were more demanding, and the hymns they were given to sing are accordingly more subtle and more practical. They both instruct the preachers in proper attitudes toward themselves as saints and sinners and suggest sermon content and effective public style.

Congregational adaptation of hymn I, "Christ the Friend of Sinners," would be almost impossible. The solo voice of the preacher is essential:

> 5   Outcasts of Men, to You I call,
>   Harlots and Publicans, and Thieves!
>   He spreads his Arms t'embrace you all;
>   Sinners alone his Grace receives:
>   No need of Him the Righteous have,
>   He came the Lost to seek and save!
>
> 6   Come all ye *Magdalens* in Lust,
>   Ye Ruffians fell in Murders old;
>   Repent, and live: despair and trust!
>   JESUS for you to Death was sold;
>   Tho' Hell protest, and Earth repine,
>   He died for Crimes like Yours—and Mine.

Wesley was instructing his preachers, through this hymn, in the proper appeal to a crowd and the necessary identification of preacher with people. The essential Methodist message is summarized in two stanzas, including the universal availability of salvation, the kindliness of Jesus, and the call to conversion. A model of effective dramatic flair is evident in the image of the preacher, spreading his arms like Jesus, to embrace his hearers. A measure of titillation is perhaps evident in the review of sins. (Certainly genuine Harlots, Publicans, and Thieves, Magdalens in Lust, and Ruffians fell in Murders old made up only a small fraction of the gathering addressed by any given preacher.) In short, the hymn provides a lesson for preachers in evangelical outreach, with a side note reminding them that they, too, are sinners. The hymn is almost sensational, and the role of the preacher, in its activity and noise, is far less passive than that recommended to the common believer.

Hymn LXXVII might serve the preacher either in a private

moment or as an effective public prelude to a sermon. A review of the temptations particular to preachers and a prayer for deliverance might very well inspire the listeners with sympathetic respect:

> Preserve me from my Calling's Snare,
>   And hide my simple Heart above,
> Above the Thorns of Choaking Care,
>   The gilded Baits of Worldly Love.[St. 3]

The hearers receive assurance both that the preacher was a sinner and that he was better, purer in heart, than they were. Through the hymn instrument, Wesley reminded the preacher, who reminded the people, both of his heroic duties and of the ideal otherworldliness of their leader.

The exciting activity of the call, even the prospect of martyrdom, is conveyed in hymn LXXVIII, "For a Preacher of the Gospel." (For Watts, most definitely, preaching had meant something quite different.)

> 1 O that I was as heretofore
>   When first sent forth in JESU's Name
>   I rush'd thro' every open Door,
>   And cried to All, "Behold the Lamb!"
>   Seiz'd the poor trembling Slaves of Sin,
>   And forc'd the Outcasts to come in.
>   . . . .
>
> 4 I want an even strong Desire,
>   I want a calmly-fervent Zeal,
>   To save poor Souls out of the Fire,
>   To snatch them from the Verge of Hell,
>   And turn them to the Pardning GOD,
>   And quench the Brands in JESU's Blood.
>   . . . .
>
> 7 Inlarge, inflame, and fill my Heart
>   With boundless Charity Divine,
>   So shall I all my Strength exert,
>   And love Them with a Zeal like Thine,
>   And lead them to thine open Side,
>   The Sheep, for whom their Shepherd died.
>
> 8 Or if, to serve thy Church and Thee
>   Myself be offer'd up at last,

> My Soul brought thro' the Purple Sea
>   With Those beneath the Altar cast
> Shall claim the Palm to Martyrs given,
> And mount the highest Throne in Heaven.

Sighing, longing, lamentation, and ecstatic passivity find no place in the preacher's life. Rather than quietude or ecstasy, the goal is the kind of active, noisy energy that Martha England credited to all of Wesley's hymns. While the lesson and the spirit of this hymn are different from those of congregational hymns, we may note Wesley's familiar unwillingness to exploit the strong images that he invokes, a reticence that we have attempted to associate with his relatively tension-free theology. The brand-quenching blood, the open side, and the purple sea are only mentioned in passing.

The activity and relative variety of the preacher's spiritual and daily life might encourage us to postulate that the hymns for preachers are closer to personal expression of Charles Wesley himself. The difficulty with any such assumption, with any personal-expressive reading of any hymns, is that Wesley's obvious public, didactic purpose precludes forthright personal confession. He turned naturally in these hymns, as in the others, to exemplary modeling of proper attitudes. If his own experience had deepened his understanding of either the ordinary believer's difficulties or the preacher's particular problems, so much the better; but the capturing of such feeling was only a means to another end.

The practical circumstances of the Methodist revival and its theological emphases had profoundly affected the poetry of its hymns. The veritable sanctification of emotion implied in charismatic conversion and the relief of Calvinist anxiety about the human condition and our ultimate punishment had loosed the flood of response that Watts had kept under control. No longer simply an antidote to indifference, feeling had become indistinguishable from salvation. Essential matters of faith, particularly God's kindliness toward humanity, were no longer problematic; the challenge was to provoke and sustain the necessary fervor. Believers had to be taught, through hymns, to feel desperate longing, then to draw close to Jesus and, freed from sin, to be ecstatically happy. In the hymns Wesley could give the singers roles to play, having them recite the lines of perfect, fervent faith. The variety and relative coherence of the hymns for preachers suggest that the atmosphere of the revival had placed severe limitations on hymns for the common folk.

The hymns suggest a loss of faith in literary response, in the singers' spontaneous reactions to traditional imagery or to carefully wrought tableaux. Wesley felt he had to steer with a heavier hand. While it served the purpose, his method of giving singers roles to play was relatively awkward, and it caused problems of hymn address and lost coherency. Such poetry of enthusiasm implied a breakdown in communication between poet and singers, a failure of confidence in the effects of the material. Wesley faced a very modern problem when he wrote poetry that attempted, by definition, to achieve broad public impact, at the same time that he distrusted his public to respond naturally and spontaneously to the material.

We cannot know how many singers could read or held books in their hands. The hymns seem to suggest, however, that the poetry was not meant for intent review. That the singers were not literate is implied in the frequent failure of syntax and the combined images. Line-by-line impact seems to have mattered most, and the total weight of accumulated imagery was apparently more important than its overall pattern. If this was indeed the case, we see in yet another instance how the circumstances of the revival affected the development of the hymn. Certainly the hymns for preachers provide an important contrast. Book-bound literature for literate singers demanded more careful composition. No less fervent, it had to sustain its ideas from stanza to stanza.

At first reading, the Wesley hymns appear to be more spontaneous and emotional than the work of Watts. The fact that John adapted devotional lyrics as hymn texts seems to reinforce this opinion. Upon closer examination, however, we see that, while the *religion* of the Wesley brothers was highly emotional, the *hymn* was calculated and controlled, an evangelical tool, precisely used to encourage the people to express those emotions that led to, then testified to, conversion. This didactic subjectivity in the hymn has little if anything to do with any spontaneous overflow of powerful feelings or with any anticipation of Wordsworth. Rather, we move even further from any probable identification of hymn with devotional lyric or with private confessional literature.

Wesley's hymns bear an intriguing relationship to the literary trends of his day. The educational purpose and exemplary method faintly recall the exemplary thrust of the contemporary novels of

Richardson. The broken speech patterns and accumulations of imagery indicate commitment to a sort of naturalistic expression. Both fervent rhapsody and quiet meditative monologues demanded psychological perspicuity. The exemplary passions had to ring true, a requirement that led the poet to experiment with sighs and groans and interrupted thoughts. Although the hymns were hardly confessional stream of consciousness, which the didactic-exemplary purpose prevents, they nevertheless depended for their success on their convincing reproduction of strong feeling. The literature of enthusiasm, by nature, must demonstrate how the bounds of language are overwhelmed by experience of the suprarational. The emotional nature of the conversion experience justified the indulgence in feeling, making it an important part of the charismatic process. Such a freedom to feel, along the recommended lines, was pleasurable, certainly, though hardly an anticipation of romanticism. The joyful tears of sentimental comedy and the appeal of melancholy through the ages evidence a similar pleasure.

A system that includes human emotion is not necessarily irrational, nor is it out of place in the eighteenth century. Wesley's hymns, like sentimental literature and a great deal of nonsentimental literature as well, encourage us to appreciate the great effort of the age to understand the working of the human mind, including the emotions. That this psychological study usually served another end—moral improvement or charismatic revival—need not invalidate its achievement. The only misfortune is the inevitably ephemeral nature of poetry, however perceptive, that distrusts its own power to communicate. The powerful feelings of the Methodist hymns appear to be scattershot fired into a diverse crowd, in contrast to Watts's silver bullet.

John Newton,
Olney Prophet

Newton at Olney

The title of the *Olney Hymns,* in its "local habitation," suggests the characteristics of John Newton's best work. These are the hymns that convey the exciting adventure of Christian life, both the individual daily variety and existence in its larger eschatological frame, and demonstrate Newton's compassionate understanding of the perfect suitability of the Gospel message to his poor, struggling singers. A new kind of hymn, essentially simpler if no easier to write, was devised for a setting and a time in which neither the theatrical tableaux and devotional sensibility of Watts nor the revivalistic enthusiasm of Wesley was appropriate. While Newton's comprehensive vision of life's larger significance and the concern for common humanity that distinguish his better hymns suggest a new poetic age, his frequent hymn failures are also instructive. The tedium and pedantry of his worst efforts illustrate the challenge of any hymn writing and the particular challenges of hymns for Newton's singers. Didactic purpose may inform or subvert the poetry of hymns. The alliance is never completely problem free. Transparently simple language may be either magnificent or dully prosaic. Sustaining a hymn voice that is truly suitable for congregational song, whether individual-universal or communal, is a hard test of the poet's control of the medium. Newton's hymns, good and bad, demonstrate that, contrary to his own theories, good hymns are good and particularly demanding poetry, not mere versification, entailing the perfect coming together of natural-seeming expression, precise image, and useful lesson, suited for congregational song.

Like those of Watts and Wesley, Newton's hymns were written in response to the particular needs of a particular situation. More than the hymns of Watts and Wesley, they bear the stamp of Newton's own experience, both before and after his conversion, suggesting the usefulness of a brief biographical survey. Newton provided an account of his extraordinary life in the *Authentic Narrative,* designed to glorify God for his mercy and power by describing his providential dealings with an exceptional sinner—an interpretation of his autobiography that figures prominently in the hymns as it emphasizes both Newton's conviction of God's intervention in human affairs and his understanding of his own experience as paradigmatic.[1] At the age of eleven, Newton had begun a career at sea, voyaging with his father. He met with many bizarre adventures in the years that followed. While still a youth, he was press-ganged, flogged for desertion, and used as a slave in Africa. Reading Shaftesbury's *Characteristics,* Newton began to doubt, and he eventually lost his faith. The moral restraints associated with religion were loosened, and according to his own account, he plumbed the depths of vice and depravity. He was rescued by reading Thomas à Kempis and by a narrow escape from drowning. Now the captain of slave ships, he tried to weld together his life and belief by spiritually uplifting his men. Finding the set prayers inappropriate for his crew, he wrote his own, even adapting the *Book of Common Prayer* to suit the situation on his ship. Newton's restless intellectual energy, his experience as an adventurer, and his familiarity with common humanity provided a distinctive education.[2]

In 1754, when he was twenty-nine, Newton left the sea and, the following year, became tide surveyor of Liverpool. He attended both Anglican and dissenting churches, and also listened to the preaching of George Whitefield, who greatly influenced his thinking. He read widely in theology and devotional literature. Convinced of God's direct intervention in his life, especially in his escapes from death, Newton felt himself chosen by God for some high purpose. As God had "redeemed me from the house of bondage in Africa, and . . . selected me as a pattern of grace to the chief of sinners," Newton determined to become a minister.[3]

Ordination, however, was not his for the asking. He was considered "eclectic" in some Anglican circles, as his association with dissenters and Methodists might suggest. Moreover, he lacked a university education. John Wesley suggested he become an itinerant preacher, but Newton felt that a congregation should be more than a group of people temporarily gathered to hear him speak. For a time he served as a visiting Congregational minister. In 1764, helped by Lord Dartmouth, who had been moved by Newton's *Authentic Narrative,* he was finally ordained into the Anglican church and was offered the curacy of Olney in Buckinghamshire. The history of Newton's ordination illustrates both the fluidity of denominations in his day and the extent to which politics could influence ordination requirements. Newton's preference for the Church of England and a proper parish are characteristic.

Newton's confidence and zeal were needed at Olney, a depressed and depressing place. It was one of the chief towns of Buckinghamshire, and its main industry, lace making, was carried on by women and children working in crowded, ill-lit rooms. The men did farm work when it was available, but family incomes were very low, and hardship and alcoholism were very common. The high incidence of blindness and madness was probably the result of the execrable working conditions. Soon after his arrival, Newton started Sunday schools for the children and weekly meetings for the adults. The *Olney Hymns* were designed for these meetings, and we may see in them Newton's attempt to supply the very real needs of this congregation for spiritual assurance, doctrinal instruction, and virtuous pleasure.

In keeping with his confidence in both the grace of God and his own special calling (and following the example of the Apostle Paul), Newton grounded his hymns in his own experience. He justified his autobiographical method in his preface: "As the workings of the heart of man, and of the Spirit of God, are in general the same in all who are the subjects of grace, I hope most of these Hymns, being the fruit and expression of my own experience, will coincide with the views of real christians of all denominations."[4] To the extent that he is a human being and a Christian, his personal experience is indeed general rather than private. Far from relying on fortuitous coincidence, the poet who would write hymns based on his own life must clearly select the sort of experience and devotional response that is commonplace and can be shared generally. That is to say, the extent to which the hymns will, in fact, suit the "views of real christians of all denominations" is a function of Newton's ability to distinguish between the universal and the idiosyncratic. (Watts, too, had begun with common sentiments.)

Newton's unique biography is, theoretically, less significant than his compassionate understanding of his singers, which provided the common standard.

The autobiographical impetus, restrained as it is supposed to be by general usefulness, suggests Newton's difference from Watts and Wesley and the rightness of his collaboration with William Cowper. Newton's most remarkable hymns are fired by a vision of Christian experience that begins with Newton's conviction of God's providential intervention in his own life and proceeds to sweep across history. The mythic self of the preacher encompasses both John Newton's calling, as he understood it, and the efforts of all priests and prophets through time. A fire or earthquake at Olney, evidence of God's active wrath and the power of the prayers of the faithful, is charged as well with biblical significance, representing a type of the final conflagration and earth shaking at the end of time. The American War, similarly, is an act of God. When Britain is identified with Israel, Old Testament precedents reinforce Newton's prophesying. The moral realm, concerning the "Rise, Progress, Changes, and Comforts of the Spiritual Life," is similarly action filled. Newton depicts Christian life as an adventure story, a courtroom drama, or a battlefield. The large, grim figure of Satan moves on earth. When Newton's prophetic imagination seized on the high drama of Christian experience through all time, he provided his singers with a large spectacle in which he himself, as individual, and they themselves, in their daily lives, had important roles to play.

Nevertheless, the majority of Newton's hymns are flawed by his inability to subordinate his clerical self-consciousness to the hymn-writing task. This is, ultimately, the same self-consciousness that provoked Newton to see spiritual significance in every item of daily life. In too many hymns, however, we hear the preacher address his flock from the pulpit, a kind of address that is fundamentally unsuitable for congregational song. "I" signifies Newton; "you" are his parishioners. This form of address can only succeed when the preacher sees himself as an exemplary saint or sinner, whose experience is no different in kind from that of his people, when his relationship to the singers is no different from their relationships to their other acquaintance. For example, in the lines "Sinners, this healing fountain try, / Which cleans'd a wretch so vile as I," it is possible to hear the Christian addressing the world in general.[5] More commonly, the preacher's voice signifies a sermon-hymn, the presence of a mixed genre that is highly problematical as congregational song. Newton's sermon-hymns fall into three parts: the text (which may be a Bible story or a general truth or observation), an explanation of the relevance of the text to the lives of the singers, and then a prayer. Newton sacrificed many hymns to this formula, which, in its lack of subtlety, is essentially prosaic as well as unsuitable for communal song.

The most interesting sermon-hymns are not based on biblical texts but rather are written within the emblem tradition. In these a rainbow, a tolling bell, a house of clay, a lodestone, a spider and a bee, a tamed lion, a sheep, or dreams are contemplated for their yield of metaphorical significance, for their emblematic truth. The metaphysical tradition determined Newton's choice and imaginative explication of his emblems, and seventeenth-century meditations, particularly those of John Donne, appear to have had their influence. Newton treated nature similarly. The seasons are exploited for their emblematic significance, as are summer storms, hay-time, harvest, thunder, lightning, an eclipse, moonlight, the sea, flooding, and thaw. With one or two exceptions, in which the real farm world of Olney seems to creep in, these phenomena are described only to the degree necessary for the homiletic purpose.

These sermon-hymns are disappointing poems. Material seemingly conducive to great poetry lies undeveloped as Newton's role as preacher supersedes his role as hymn-writer. While, in their use of emblem and typology, the sermon-hymns illustrate Newton's sense that the world is packed with signs and messages from God, in their limitation to formulas that fail to integrate sign and meaning, they illustrate his inadequacies as a poet. Newton's signs rarely materialize as images or poetic figures; they remain mere evidence.

Although visionary hymns would seem to demand the best poetry possible, Newton shared Watts's opinion that hymns should be conceptually simple and should be stripped of distracting decoration. Their agreement proceeds from very different quarters:

There is a style and manner suited to the composition of Hymns, which may be more successfully, or at least more easily, attained by a versifier than by a poet. They should be Hymns, not Odes, if designed for public worship, and for the use of plain people. Perspicuity simplicity, and ease, should be chiefly attended to; and the imagery and colouring of poetry, if admitted at all, should be indulged very sparingly, and with great judgment.[6]

In our consideration of Watts's ambivalence toward poetry, we noted that imaginative restraint, inspired by the spirit of ascetic denial, was at odds with the commitment to the power of poetry that motivated him to write poetry in the first place. Watts had worried that imaginative flights would distract the singers, implying that poetry was easier to follow than devotion. Newton, in a different time and place, calls for restraint for very different reasons. Far from pleasant distraction, the danger of poetry had become its inaccessibility to ordinary folk. The sermon-hymns provided little distraction.

Within a narrow range of hymn subject matter that has definite imaginative relevance to his view of himself and of Olney, Newton excelled as a hymn writer. In these hymns he avoided preaching and transcended mere versification. Here, too, the strength of belief and clarity of vision are complemented by the simplicity and restraint that he advocated. With Newton's biography in mind, a life story certainly familiar to his parishioners, we see in "Amazing Grace" (XLI) Newton's hymn writing at its best advantage. The transparent language summarizes experience shared by poet and singers, clarifying for all the importance of grace:

> 1 Amazing grace! (how sweet the sound!)
>   That sav'd a wretch like me!
>   I once was lost, but now am found,
>   Was blind, but now I see.
>
> 2 'Twas grace that taught my heart to fear,
>   And grace my fears reliev'd;
>   How precious did that grace appear,
>   The hour I first believ'd.
>
> 3 Through many dangers, toils, and snares,
>   I have already come;
>   'Tis grace has brought me safe thus far,
>   And grace will lead me home.
>
> 4 The Lord has promis'd good to me,
>   His word my hope secures;
>   He will my shield and portion be,
>   As long as life endures.

> 5 Yea, when this heart and flesh shall fail,
>   And mortal life shall cease;
>   I shall possess, within the vail,
>   A life of joy and peace.
>
> 6 The earth shall soon dissolve like snow,
>   The sun forbear to shine;
>   But God, who call'd me here below,
>   Will be for ever mine.

The facts of wretchedness, lostness, and blindness, of dangers, toils, and snares, and the distance from home, in Newton's life at sea and in his people's present, cancel the need for the sort of metaphorical interpretation typical of Wesley's hymns. Grace is almost personified as a kindly, motherly deity, who cares for the sinner as a lost child, but Newton characteristically stops short of even this poetic figure. Also in contrast to Wesley's hymns, the human soul has not become passive but rather continues on its troubled way, secure in hope and confident of the power and benevolence of God. Newton's best hymns, practical and immediate, derive their power from just such a successful identification, in all humility, of poet with singers.

In hymn LXIX, the elect members of the Olney congregation are encouraged to contrast their state with the damnation of the "worldlings." As the singers learn to count their spiritual blessings and to enjoy the prospect of future bliss, they also learn to cope with the temporal humiliation of the poor. As in "Amazing Grace," Newton's life story provides him with a special authority, and he begins the hymn "From pole to pole let others roam, / And search in vain for bliss." He proceeds to lead his people in an exemplary acclamation of the Lord's sufficiency with special reference to the pangs of poverty:

> Let worldlings then indulge their boast,
>   How much they gain or spend;
> Their joys must soon give up the ghost,
>   But mine shall know no end. [St. 6]

Hymns for truly poor and humble Christians *may* be straightforward; they need neither the metaphorical translation into spiritual hunger and humility so frequently found in Wesley's hymns nor the aesthetic and intellectual jolt of Watts. Sensibility, after all, is recognized by scholars as an essentially middle-class phenomenon. The damned, in

Newton's hymns, are those genuinely "wretched . . . and blind, and poor, / And dying while they live"(LIV). The singers, temporarily miserable, may understand the contrast between their material poverty and the spiritual poverty of the worldlings, secure in the promise that they themselves will be revealed in the end as blessed:

> Assembled worlds will then discern
> The saints alone are blest;
> When wrath shall like an oven burn,
> And vengeance strike the rest. [LXXX, 6]

The perfect suitability of the unadorned Gospel message, with its Lazarus and its rich man (CV), its poor widow (XXXVI), and its debtors (XCVIII), to the poor lace makers of Olney gave Newton a remarkable advantage.

Newton's excellence in this simple, direct mode contrasts sharply with the tedium of many of his less inspired doctrinal and Bible story hymns. In these he settles for a sermon model and mere versification. Watts and Wesley had, each in his own way, risen to the literary challenge of making a variety of dogmatic points and of rendering many different Bible stories in memorable verse. Newton's difficulty demonstrates the accomplishment of his predecessors as well as his own limitations. Describing the reconciliation and restoration of sinners through grace, for example, Newton is unable to fire his hymn with the specific expression of general experience that he had so successfully realized in "Amazing Grace." He began hymn XXIX of book II from the pulpit:

> 1   Alas! by nature how deprav'd,
>   How prone to ev'ry ill!
>   Our lives to Satan how enslav'd,
>   How obstinate our will!
>
> 2   And can such sinners be restor'd,
>   Such rebels reconcil'd?
>   Can grace itself the means afford,
>   To make a foe a child?

He has settled for versified sermonettes. The direct affirmation and subtle lesson of "Amazing Grace" have been sacrificed to rhetorical question and pedantic pronouncement. Newton frequently failed in this fashion to reconcile the instructive and the literary obligations of the hymn writer.

Hymn LXXXIX was designed to lead the singers through the arguments necessary to refute the errors of other religious sects. The first stanza stresses the need for belief in the divinity of Christ: "You cannot be right in the rest, / Unless you think rightly of him." In the following stanza, the singer responds to those who consider Christ a mere man or angel:

> I durst not confide in his blood,
> Nor on his protection rely,
> Unless I were sure he is God.

Then the necessity of grace for salvation and the inefficacy of good works are contrasted with works-righteousness: "Some call him a Saviour, in word, / But mix their own works with his plan." The educational job is being done, certainly, but the product, devoid of any kind of poetic imagination, is hardly a hymn.

The final stanza of the same hymn contrasts sharply with the preliminary material. The singers are turned from their doctrinal review to a positive affirmation of what they do indeed believe, releasing a flood of suggestion and real poetry:

> If ask'd, what of Jesus I think?
> Though still my best thoughts are but poor,
> I say, He's my meat and my drink,
> My life, and my strength, and my store;
> My shepherd, my husband, my friend,
> My Saviour from sin and from thrall;
> My hope from beginning to end,
> My portion, my Lord, and my all.

When Newton exploits the domestic images of meat and drink, of husband and friend, relating the vitality of faith to the singers' everyday experience, the hymn comes to life as poetry. The rush of analogy is acceptable, rather than confusing, because it illustrates, as intended, the "All-ness" of Jesus.

The nature of Newton's achievement in his best hymns is clarified by one of his most famous, "The Name of Jesus" (LVII). Its virtues are those of the last stanza of the above. Pedestrian expression and dull versification are entirely absent from this simple and moving statement of the comfort brought by faith. The theological lesson is skillfully interwoven, reinforcing the emotional integrity of the hymn:

1   How sweet the name of Jesus sounds
        In a believer's ear!
    It soothes his sorrows, heals his wounds,
        And drives away his fear.

2   It makes the wounded spirit whole,
        And calms the troubled breast;
    'Tis manna to the hungry soul,
        And to the weary rest.

3   Dear name! the rock on which I build,
        My shield and hiding-place;
    My never-failing treasury, fill'd
        With boundless stores of grace.

4   By thee my prayers acceptance gain,
        Although with sin defil'd;
    Satan accuses me in vain,
        And I am own'd a child.

5   Jesus! my Shepherd, Husband, Friend,
        My Prophet, Priest, and King!
    My Lord, my Life, my Way, my End!
        Accept the praise I bring.

6   Weak is the effort of my heart,
        And cold my warmest thought;
    But when I see thee as thou art,
        I'll praise thee as I ought.

7   Till then I would thy love proclaim
        With ev'ry fleeting breath;
    And may the music of thy name
        Refresh my soul in death!

The hymn suggests that the objective, third-person approach of its own first two stanzas is inadequate. The address shifts significantly, from a fairly cool series of metaphors to direct address using the name of Jesus. Strong feeling and restraint work together, however, controlling the ecstatic potential of this hymn. In the first two stanzas, the sufficiency of Jesus for all needs, spiritual and corporeal, lends substance to the "sweetness" of his name, illustrating the solid completeness of salvation. Likewise, in the third stanza, the "dear" name is immediately buttressed by the bulk and protection of the rock and the shield, the hiding place and the treasury. Indulgence in sentiment is avoided, a reminder of the discipline of the Olney parish, as the singers' phyusical misery is reflected in every stanza, in their sorrows, wounds, fears' trouble, hunger, weariness; vulnerability and poverty, alienation and orphanhood; weakness, coldness, blindness; and mortality, respectively. The balance of specific poetry and exemplary instruction is evident throughout.

Newton's self-confessed "mediocrity of talent" cannot explain the discrepancy between his very good and his very bad hymns. A poor poet could not have produced "Amazing Grace" or "The Name of Jesus." Yet we may marvel that a good poet could have sent the tediously uninspired, pedantic stanzas to the printer. One explanation would seem to derive from the dependence of hymns on nonhymn literary models. Newton was ill at ease when he wrote didactic hymns to the degree that didactic poetry was out of fashion. The great didactic hymn models had been written many decades earlier, during the age of Augustan verse, with its Horatian ideals. Charles Wesley had managed to replace the limpid precision of Augustan verse with exemplary charismatic sensibility and the dramatic flurry of the revival. Neither approach really suited Newton's cast of mind or his people's needs. Not surprisingly, in his overtly didactic hymns, he turned to the most obvious literary model, which was the sermon. That sermon-hymns were basically unsatisfactory as poetry evidently did not deter him.

Most of Newton's Bible story hymns, like his dogmatic-confessional hymns, fall victim to the sermon formula. In the initial stanzas, he tells the story. The narrative, generally an uninspired verse paraphrase, is followed by its application, signaled by "thus" or "so we" or "like him" or even "nor is it a singular case." A short prayer follows. This standard format is seen in hymn V:

> 1 How hurtful was the choice of Lot,
>   Who took up his abode

> (Because it was a fruitful spot)
> With them who fear'd not God!
>
> 2 A pris'ner he was quickly made,
>   Bereav'd of all his store;
>   And, but for Abram's timely aid,
>   He had return'd no more.

The narrative continues for five more stanzas. The eighth then applies the message to the singers and provides a short prayer:

> The doom of Sodom will be ours,
> If to the earth we cleave;
> Lord, quicken all our drowsy powers,
> To flee to thee, and live.

These hymns offer only the unadorned metrical adaptation of story to music, a moral application, and a little prayer. Occasionally Newton enlivens his subject with fictional detail (Cain, in II, has a "sullen downcast look") or attempts a bit of dialogue, but in the main we are kept very close to the detail and language of the Bible.[7]

In the final prayer of the hymns written to the sermon formula, Newton sometimes achieves the real integration of image and lesson we expect of poetry—and of hymns. He would better have begun a new hymn with his final stanza. In "Disciples at Sea," for example, after the doggerel of four stanzas of narrative, Newton wrote:

> Yet, Lord, we are ready to shrink,
> Unless we thy presence perceive;
> O save us, we cry, or we sink,
> We would, but we cannot believe.
> The night has been long and severe,
> The winds and the seas are still high;
> Dear Saviour, this moment appear,
> And say to our souls, "It is I!"[CXIV]

Perhaps, given the deprivation at Olney, Newton could not assume that his singers would be familiar with either Scripture or Christian doctrine, and therefore he could not exploit that fund of common understanding and imagery upon which poetry perforce must draw.

When he was able to integrate a particular Bible story with his own dearest convictions and the life experience of the singers, Newton avoided the sermon formula and wrote much more imaginatively. The most appealing biblical hymns place the singers in the story, not by means of one or two moral stanzas, but through total identification of the biblical situation with the singers' experience. In hymn XIII we taste the bitter waters of Exodus, flowing through the desert of our lives:

> 1 Bitter, indeed, the waters are,
>   Which in this desert flow;
> Though to the eye they promise fair,
>   They taste of sin and woe.
>
> 2 Of pleasing draughts I once could dream,
>   But now, awake, I find
> That sin has poison'd ev'ry stream,
>   And left a curse behind.

The universal experience of lost illusion and the poisonous aftermath of sin, and the promise of relief in the cross, bring the story to life. Newton could not do the same thing for the "choice of Lot" and the "doom of Sodom." When he was struck by the genuine familiarity of a particular scene, Newton could and did enter his singers into the biblical action in the traditional manner of Watts and Wesley. In hymn XLIV, the singers become Job, mocked by Satan: "Satan asks, and mocks my woe, / 'Boaster, where is now your God?' " Presumably the singers knew more of satanic scorn than of Joseph's fraternal forgiveness.

After a single, awkward, introductory stanza in hymn XCIX, the singer becomes the wounded traveler in the parable of the Good Samaritan:

> Men saw me in this helpless case,
> And pass'd without compassion by:
> Each neighbour turn'd away his face,
> Unmoved by my mournful cry. [St. 3]

Jesus is the Good Samaritan; the inn is the church. Most significantly, the relevance of the story to "real life" is presumed and enjoyed rather than explicated. Newton's sensitivity to the substantial sufferings of his people and to the substantial deliverance offered by God, which characterizes his best work, determines which biblical narratives will come to dramatic life.

Newton's biography and the Olney setting provide more than mere background to his hymns. In his hymn failures he seems to have been following dutifully in the footsteps of his predecessors, without a real talent for didactic poetry and across a difficult terrain, given the limitations of the Olney singers. Moreover, for Newton, instruction in the faith was the task of the preacher, not of the poet, and his sermon-hymns are accordingly prosaic. Perhaps the fine tableaux of Watts were unsuited to Olney and neither the yearning nor the ecstasy of Wesley's hymns provided the continuous comfort needed by Newton's flock. Newton, as pastor, seized on the particular truths and biblical scenes that fitted his vision and purpose, producing hymns that distinguish themselves as poetry. He also versified quantities of biblical material and doctrinal instruction for merely educational ends. These verses demonstrate how easily the unimaginative hymns, with their metrical limitations and their failure to exploit the power of language to suggest and explain profound meaning, can degenerate into doggerel.

History & Prophecy

The poetic power that animates Newton's best hymns is more than an occasional high indicating the discovery of the special relevance of a particular hymn subject. The good hymns also manifest Newton's highly individual vision of spiritual reality, seen in his autobiography and suggested by the emblematic meditations. Life in this world, both private and public, is patterned by Providence and is hence replete with religious significance. God's revelation is continual. Piety, asceticism, and ecstasy are not particularly important. The impulse that led Newton to see himself as God's illustration of his grace for the benefit of all people also inclined Newton to magnify all experience to mythic proportions. He projected on a large screen, as it were, the imposing, oversize figures of Satan, Olney, Britain, and the preacher. Personal redemption, daily life at Olney, and current international events are all on the same scale, all signs of divine purpose and essentially no different from the experience recorded in the Old and New Testaments.

Newton's feeling for the stirring drama of daily Christian life in this world complements his charitable concern for the miserable human lot of his singers:

> 1   Though troubles assail,
>   And dangers affright,
>   Though friends should all fail,
>   And foes all unite;
>   Yet one thing secures us,
>   Whatever betide,
>   The scripture assures us,
>   The LORD will provide.
>
> 2   The birds without barn
>   Or storehouse are fed;
>   From them let us learn
>   To trust for our bread:
>   His saints, what is fitting,
>   Shall ne'er be denied,
>   So long as 'tis written,
>   The LORD will provide.
>
> 3   We may, like the ships,
>   By tempests be tossed,
>   On perilous deeps,
>   But cannot be lost:
>   Though Satan enrages
>   The wind and the tide,
>   The promise engages,
>   The LORD will provide. [VII]

The guarantee of divine sustenance applies to the everyday dinner tables at Olney and to the dangerous, if less specific, buffetings of life. The singer-parishioner's familiarity with Newton's own ordeals at sea reinforces the imagery. Metaphorical clarity and exemplary assurance together allow Newton to overcome his tendency to lecture his singers.

The figure of Satan looms large in almost all of the hymns that successfully treat the struggles of Christian life. "Though troubles assail" proceeds to tell of the appearances of Satan and his arguments, all of which may be answered by "This heart-cheering promise, / The

LORD will provide." The satanic presence regularly lifts a hymn above the tedious norm, particularly in the largely scriptural first book. The hymn "Elijah Fed by Ravens," for example, has all the prosaic limitations of the sermon-hymns, beginning "Elijah's example declares," until the image of Satan as raven captures Newton's imagination:

> Thus Satan, that raven unclean,
> Who croaks in the ears of the saints,
> Compell'd by a power unseen,
> Administers oft to their wants;
> God teaches them how to find food,
> From all the temptations they feel:
> This raven who thirsts for my blood,
> Has help'd me to many a meal. [XXXV, 4]

No mere analogy, the bird-Satan is living and familiar.

Satanic responsibility for all things threatening and evil, in both the physical and the moral worlds, allows Newton a simple mythology of good and evil and allows God to exercise unmitigated kindliness. (William Cowper's much more complex vision permitted no such polarization.) In a vivid courtroom drama in hymn LXXVII, Satan is the "fierce foe," the insulting accuser, ultimately rebuked by the almighty and forgiving Judge. Elsewhere, "always nigh, / To tear and to destroy," he lies in wait for the weakening soul or openly fights against the walled citadel of the elect (CVIII). In the third book, "on the rise, progress, changes, and comforts of the spiritual life," hymns addressed to particularly wicked sinners remind them of "Satan's dark dwelling, / The prison beneath" (I). The substantial reality of satanic power, now and in the end, enlivens the drama of this life as battleground for the soul.

This hymn writer, who had such difficulty bringing the stories of Lot and Joseph to life, provides a fine account of the struggle of good and evil, Jesus and Satan, for the soul:

> When Jesus claims the sinner's heart,
>   Where Satan ruled before;
> The evil spirit must depart,
>   And dares return no more. [LXXXIV, 1]

The superior claim of Jesus cannot protect the reformed individual from backsliding, however, and Satan has considerable power over the imperfect Christian:

> With rage, and malice seven-fold,
>   He then resumes his sway,
> No more by checks to be control'd,
>   No more to go away. [St. 5]

The hymn suggests that, our chance once lost, we are abandoned to the despair that is Satan's last gift. The liveliness of Satan and his active participation in human affairs provided both simple edification and "entertainment" at Olney. Satan was more familiar, hence more poetically accessible without extensive exposition, than many other biblical figures. He was an item in the common fund of culture, while Lot presumably was not.

A second kind of hymn that rises above the prosaic norm concerns the spiritual significance of current events, at Olney, in England, and in the world at large. Oversize, active, mythic personifications march at the Lord's command, in this world, here and now. The singing faithful are involved in this historical drama by virtue of their special status as the elect of the Lord. An Olney incident that achieves special dramatic treatment is the fire that broke out in the town and destroyed many houses. The fire becomes, not surprisingly, God's punishment, visited on Olney for ingratitude and sin: "He spoke at last, / And bid the fire rebuke our sin:"

> But prayer prevail'd and sav'd the town:
> The few who lov'd the Saviour's name
> Were heard, and mercy hasted down
> To change the wind and stop the flame. [II, LXIX, 7]

The small company of the elect may pride itself on having saved the wicked town from general conflagration. The people's safety from the vengeance of the Lord is the presence in their midst of the elect, a heroic role for the community of the faithful:

> 7 The gospel, and a praying few,
>   Our bulwark long have prov'd;

> But Olney sure the day will rue
> When these shall be remov'd.

8   Then sin, in this once-favour'd town,
   Will triumph unrestrain'd;
And wrath and vengeance hasten down,
   No more by prayer detain'd. [II, XLIX]

Olney, identified with the biblical towns of the Old Testament, is threatened with divine retribution, while the people of God are given the exhilarating responsibility of saving their neighbors from the wrath of God.[8]

The church plays an important role in Newton's Christian drama; the emphasis on its sustaining function is appropriate for an Anglican curate and is absent from the hymns of the Independent, Watts, and of Wesley, the field preacher. In hymn II, XII, the steps of life and the dangers attendant on each are traced. At every step, Christ expresses himself through the church and is present to help and to save. In II, LI, the church is viewed as a garden, in need of the Lord's "gracious rain," lest its members, like neglected plants, "droop and die." This church is not an abstract entity but rather the community known first hand by the singers: if Newton had been writing about an abstract church, he would have lectured his singers.

Newton also served his people, through the hymns, as a prophetic news commentator, interpreting the events of the larger world to them as packed with divine significance. War in America, like the Olney fire, manifested the direct intervention of God in human affairs: "See, how war, with dreadful stride, / Marches at the Lord's command" (II, V). The subject inspired Newton to the creation of impressive tableaux much more stirring, certainly, than the versifications of Bible stories. War and plague are inflated and are decorated as frightening characters, anticipating Blake's more-than-personifications in *America*.[9] Like the figure of Satan, they deflect blame for cosmic evil and vengeance away from God:

> See, how war, with dreadful stride,
> Marches at the Lord's command,
> Spreading desolation wide,
> Through a once much favour'd land:
> War, with heart and arms of steel,
> Preys on thousands at a meal;

> Daily drinking human gore,
> Still he thirsts and calls for more. [St. 3]

Like the Olney fire, divine punishment by war can only be averted by the prayers of the faithful.

The large canvas of current events suited Newton's taste for mythic magnification. Hymn II, LXVII, "The Hiding-Place," makes a startling connection between the war and Olney. In the first stanza, we are called to watch the approaching storm of war, a storm figuring all at once the biblical menace of Isaiah, the menace of war in England, and the threat of individual damnation:

> See the gloomy gath'ring cloud
> Hanging o'er a sinful land!
> Sure the Lord proclaims aloud
> Times of trouble are at hand.

God speaks, revealing to the singers as they recite the words, that he has prepared a hiding place for them that is secure from the destruction to come, which is aimed at the rest of the sinful country:

> "You have only to repose
> On my wisdom, love, and care;
> When my wrath consumes my foes,
> Mercy shall my children spare:
> While they perish in the flood,
> You that bear my holy mark,
> Sprinkled with atoning blood,
> Shall be safe within the ark." [St. 3]

No hymn better demonstrates the completeness of Newton's vision, which found divine meaning in current events, saw Olney as a cosmic stage, reduced all of ethics to a struggle between the devil and the Lord, and viewed himself as God's particular message to humanity. Biblical reference, when it supports Newton's vision, adds scope and dignity to a hymn, making the idiosyncratic message seem less so.[10]

Two sorts of poetically energized hymn, then, treat the activity of Satan and the transhistorical tableaux of Providence. A third kind centers on Newton himself. As the pastor of this particular flock and as representational soul, he played an important part in his own hymn drama, particularly in a number of hymns that treat the special place of Newton as preacher in the divine order. Newton evidently felt that, like Satan and Providence, he was himself as priest a familiar item of his people's religious experience. We know from the *Authentic Narrative* that Newton considered himself "one of the most astonishing instances of the forbearance and mercy of God upon the face of the earth," and we have seen him, in "Amazing Grace" and a few other hymns, transform this representational status into the persona of broadly appealing, eminently congregational songs. This transformation did not always take place, however, and in many of Newton's hymns, even when he avoids the sermon formula, personal expression overwhelms the public purpose of the verses.

On occasion, we are forcefully reminded of Newton the author: "Though of sinners I am chief, / He has rank'd me with his saints" recalls the preeminence in sin claimed by Newton in his autobiography. It certainly loses some of its force as the claim of every singer in the congregation. In II, LII, "Hoping for a Revival," we sing the misery of the spiritual leader as hymn writer who cannot compose and then the happiness he knows when Christ speaks to him and revives his powers:

> 1 My harp untun'd and laid aside,
>   (To cheerful hours the harp belongs)
>   My cruel foes insulting cried,
>   "Come, sing us one of Zion's songs."

Although Newton did not play the harp, of course David did, and the identification is not idle. The cruel and insulting foes enhance the heroic quality of the hymn writer, who has Christ on his side. The Savior answers:

> 6 "Take down thy long-neglected harp,
>   I've seen thy tears, and heard thy prayer,
>   The winter-season has been sharp,
>   But spring shall all its wastes repair."

The hymnist then turns to his people to lead them in song:

> 7 Lord, I obey; my hopes revive;
>   Come, join with me, ye saints, and sing,

> Our foes in vain against us strive,
> For God will help and healing bring.

Perhaps Newton had failed to provide his usual new hymns to his people for several weeks, and he was announcing the resumption of the custom. Whatever the circumstances, the hymn does not transcend them. It is one hymn writer's apology to his congregation.

Wesley had written hymns for preachers as spiritual leaders with special needs. Those hymns feature the dramatic possibilities of the preacher's role, his activity in contrast to the passivity expected of his audience. But the very specificity of Olney distinguishes Newton's self-conscious depiction of the place of the preacher; the hymns are written with reference to himself, a personalism at odds with the character of the congregational hymn as we have defined it in the work of Watts and Wesley. Certainly the congregational base of the Olney hymns, the specificity of so much material to Olney, encouraged this use of the pastor as hymn focus because he was, ex officio, a part of every singer's religious life. It is also possible that Newton's struggle for ordination and his conviction of his own importance as a divine illustration left him with a need to restate and reaffirm, for his people, his place in the tradition of Old and New Testament prophets and priests, as a means of legitimizing his authority.

The singer, as preacher, repeatedly identifies himself with his biblical predecessors. In II, XIII, Elisha's powerlessness without God's support is compared with the modern cry: "Lord, we have tried and tried again, / We find them dead, and leave them so." The power is God's, the means are "our appointed part." In II, XIX, the singer-preacher asks for the mantle of Peter, as successor to Elijah and Elisha. The preacher is raised above the congregation in his assurance of salvation and in his divine mission. A latter-day prophet, he asks the Lord, "Assist thy messenger to speak."

The dramatic presentation of the preacher as prophet and priest is sometimes at odds with Newton's claim to preeminence in sin, his representational function as remarkable instance of God's grace. The preacher is cast as Ezekiel:

> Like him, around I cast my eye,
> And, oh! what heaps of bones appear;
> Like him, by Jesus sent, I'll try,
> For he can cause the dead to hear. [II, XV, 4]

The near association with God makes the identification with Ezekiel seem commonplace. The preacher as both judge and miracle worker looms large indeed.

In hymns XVI and XVII of the same book, Newton identifies the preacher with Moses and asks God for the power of his predecessor. Newton's self-abnegation and his Mosaic ambition clash in the image of a preaching worm, bearing Moses' rod:

> 4   O Lord, regard thy people's prayers!
>   Assist a worm to preach aright;
>   And since thy gospel-rod he bears,
>   Display thy wonders in our sight. [XVI]

In the following stanzas, Newton conveys to posterity the favored style of preaching and the desired response:

> 5   Proclaim the thunders of thy law,
>   Like lightning let thine arrows fly,
>   That careless sinners, struck with awe,
>   For refuge may to Jesus cry!
>
> 6   Make streams of godly sorrow flow
>   From rocky hearts, unus'd to feel;
>   And let the poor in spirit know,
>   That thou art near, their griefs to heal.

The central place accorded the sermon assured the status of the preacher in the community.

The following hymn, in a similar vein, asks God to work with the preacher and to lend him power, "Yet, till almighty power constrain, / This matchless love is preach'd in vain." Paradoxically, such humble deference to the source of preaching power exalts the preacher even further, as his power and success in the pulpit become proofs of divine favor and support.

We have noted that Newton's most inspired hymns have considerable visual appeal; their descriptive effort succeeds. When his imagination was fired by the vital importance of a subject and when he could trust his singers to appreciate his references, the verses become poetry. The Bible stories that transcend verse paraphrase are those that relate to such a vision and permit such a trust. Among Newton's preacher hymns, similarly, a tableau of Aaron succeeds because of the priestly figure who is central to Newton's drama of faith. The biblical character, as a type of Jesus, and the modern Anglican priest become one, familiar to the singers from Sunday worship:

> See Aaron, God's anointed priest,
> Within the vail appear,
> In robes of mystic meaning drest,
> Presenting Israel's prayer. [II, XIX, 1]

Each stanza presents a new aspect of the transhistorical Priest, who both bears "The names of all the tribes" on his shining breast and celebrates the sacrament:

> With the atoning blood he stands
> Before the mercy-seat;
> And clouds of incense from his hands
> Arise with odour sweet. [St. 3]

He imparts "the sacred light of truth . . . to teach and to adorn," and stands for Jesus, the "greater Priest" to the "eye of faith."

> The blood, which as a priest he bears
> For sinners, is his own;
> The incense of his prayers and tears
> Perfume the holy throne. [St. 8]

In his final stanza, Newton retreats from the identification, singing as a "weak and vile" individual, whose name is nonetheless inscribed on Jesus' breast.

The situation of the preacher in relation to his people enlivens the hymn interpretation of the parable of the fig tree in hymn CIII. "The church a garden is," and the believers are "ornamental trees / Planted by God's own hand," an image reflecting the divine design and natural and proper growth of creation. The infiltration of the elect circle by the damned, who are, contrary to appearances, devoid of grace, is noted by the preacher, the deputy of the true gardener, who is Christ. The preacher becomes, within the hymn, the undergardener, Christ's substitute on earth, a position of considerable power and importance. Even more striking than such an identification, the preacher is characterized as more merciful than God, as he repines at the absolute decree that consigns the fruitless to perdition; he wishes he could save them:

> 3   The under gard'ner grieves,
> In vain his strength he spends,
> For heaps of useless leaves
> Afford him small amends:
> He hears the Lord his will make known,
> To cut the barren fig-trees down.

> 4   How difficult his post,
> What pangs his bowels move,
> To find his wishes cross'd,
> His labours useless prove!
> His last relief, his earnest prayer,
> "Lord, spare them yet another year:"

God's destruction is grievous to his substitute on earth, who feels a pity beyond the divine. The undergardener wants to apply "fresh manure" to make the barren trees bear fruit—an interesting image for clerical exhortation. If "no gracious fruits appear" soon, God will strike "the threaten'd blow," possibly deferred for a time at the preacher's behest.

In hymn II, XXVI, the particular sorrows and joys of the preacher's life are reported, suggesting the practical service these hymns were designed to render. As the congregation sings, its members may learn to appreciate their minister, to see him as their heroic leader:

> 1   What contradictions meet
> In ministers employ!
> It is a bitter sweet,
> A sorrow full of joy:
> No other post affords a place,
> For equal honour or disgrace!

> 2   Who can describe the pain
> Which faithful preachers feel,
> Constrain'd to speak in vain,
> To hearts as hard as steel!
> Or who can tell the pleasures felt,
> When stubborn hearts begin to melt!

The preacher's sorrows and joys, like those of Christ in other hymns, proceed from the sins and repentance of his followers. The hymn seems calculated to inspire the congregation to want to do better, an item in pastoral public relations.

In the final stanza, Newton corrects any misconceptions he may have fostered in the earlier verses by emphasizing that the power to melt hearts is the Lord's and his the praise:

> On what has now been sown,
> Thy blessing, Lord, bestow;
> The power is thine alone,
> To make it spring and grow:
> Do thou the gracious harvest raise,
> And thou alone shalt have the praise. [St. 6]

The impression of the heroic labor of the preacher and of his importance in the salvific scheme remains.

The prominence of the preacher in Newton's hymns and his emphasis on his personal difficulties and on his special relationship to God and his people suggests a basic insecurity on Newton's part about the substance of his authority. He apparently needed to restate and reaffirm, for his people and himself, his place in the tradition of biblical prophets and priests. Beyond his clerical self-consciousness, however, whatever its biographical origins, and beyond his frequent and unfortunate turn to the sermon-hymn formula, whatever the educational deprivation at Olney, Newton's elevation of the preacher is one item of his larger vision of God active and visible in the world. This large vision provides the imaginative power that transforms mere versification into poetry. Newton took his own charismatic conversion as the example of providential intervention in human affairs and proceeded to generalize, seeing all of life as laced with spiritual significance. He did not, of course, invent the idea of Providence or the divine meaning of the Creation, and his hymns gain resonance through their references to God's relationship to Israel, to St. Paul's conversion, to traditional views of war as God's vengeance, and to the emblem tradition.

The novelty of Newton's vision lay in its charismatic, evangelical coloring. The believing self stood at the center of this visionary sweep across continents and through history, transforming ordinary perception of ordinary events and human conditions into exciting and ultimately significant manifestations of divine purpose. In the context of this large view, the awkward pivotal analogies of the sermon hymns, in which Newton applies his dogmatic point or explains the relevance of a Bible story, become more important than they might otherwise have been, as visionary moments trapped in a prosaic text.

Newton's best hymns crystallize his transhistorical vision, spanning the ages and integrating present and biblical experience in a large historical drama. Britain is Israel, known at Olney; Newton, Moses, Aaron, and Elisha are one with the Lord; the Olney fire is God's retribution no less than the slaughter of the firstborn Egyptians. This scheme has oversize roles for Satan, the Preacher, the town, and the faithful. The power Newton derived from concrete domestic reference proceeded from this vision, which endows everyday experience with ultimate significance. The familiarity of the author with the sorrows and real deprivation of his people assured a supply of realistic raw material. "Zion, or the City of God" illustrates the best of Newton and his means of achieving it:

1   Glorious things of thee are spoken,
     Zion, city of our God!
     He, whose word cannot be broken,
     Form'd thee for his own abode:
     On the Rock of ages founded,
     What can shake thy sure repose?
     With salvation's walls surrounded,
     Thou may'st smile at all thy foes.

2   See! the streams of living waters,
     Springing from eternal love,
     Well supply thy sons and daughters,
     And all fear of want remove.
     Who can faint when such a river,
     Ever flows their thirst to assuage?
     Grace, which like the Lord, the giver,
     Never fails from age to age.

3   Round each habitation hov'ring,
     See the cloud and fire appear!
     For a glory and a cov'ring,
     Shewing that the Lord is near;

> Thus deriving from their banner,
> Light by night, and shade by day:
> Safe they feed upon the manna
> Which he gives them when they pray.
>
> 4 Bless'd inhabitants of Zion,
> Wash'd in the Redeemer's blood!
> Jesus, whom their souls rely on,
> Makes them kings and priests to God.
> 'Tis his love his people raises
> Over self to reign as kings,
> And as priests, his solemn praises
> Each for a thank-off'ring brings.
>
> 5 Saviour, if of Zion's city
> I through grace a member am,
> Let the world deride or pity,
> I will glory in thy name:
> Fading is the worldling's pleasure,
> All his boasted pomp and show;
> Solid joys and lasting treasure,
> None but Zion's children know. [LX]

Each of these stanzas explains and amplifies a traditional image by means of immediately intelligible, tangible reference. The result is true poetry, not the crude versification of the less successful hymns. The city of Zion takes on the substantial reality of Olney as the faithful become citizens of Zion through the working of the hymn, showing how Newton's poetic success was contingent on the suitability of his subject to his dramatic vision.

In the first stanza the poet summarizes what we know of Zion, warming the traditional language with human experience, animating the ideas. The city of God, the rock of ages, the walls of salvation, are balanced by the more immediate human experience of square dealing, house building, undisturbed rest, and smiling security. The second stanza works similarly, as the "streams of living waters / Springing from eternal love" become vitally important to the singers through reference to ordinary fear of want and danger of fainting, while the "eternal love" is humanized by the image of the father supplying his children and the constancy of a river through the ages illustrates the unfailing grace of God.

In the third stanza, the identification of the singers with the children of Zion is completed. The houses of Olney are the habitations protected by the cloud from darkness and heat. Olney, Israel, and Zion are undistinguishable as the present, the past, and the future are one in the Lord. The call to "See" indicates the completeness of the vision. Such an identification is reinforced in the following stanza in the reference to the Christian social reversal, an important item of Newton's message to Olney, as we have seen. The redeemed, however wretched in worldly terms, become kings in their self-mastery and priests in their relationship to God. The hymn itself, as "solemn praise," attests to the priestly elevation of the believer.

The last stanza yields the lesson for the individual. The use of the first-person singular pronoun indicates the exemplary content of the lines as they tell us how to respond to our wretched lot in this life and to the pity or derision it may inspire in worldlings. We singers are indeed the fortunate ones.

Of Things to Come

For every successful hymn Newton wrote in the conventional exemplary mode, in which the singers are led through proper devotional formulations, he wrote five hymns in which the singers take lessons and lectures, as from the pulpit, in religious truth. The models of devotionally instructive verse designed by Watts and Wesley seem no longer to have served. Didactic poetry of the Watts type, with its integration of image and lesson, depended for its success on a common fund of religious reference, particularly on the singers' familiarity with the Bible and with exegetical tradition. It was not necessary for Watts to begin at the beginning. He began, rather, with common perceptions of ordinary Christians who were, actually, quite knowledgeable about "Divinity." He could assume that his singers were familiar with a whole literary tradition, both Puritan and secular, including psalms and emblems, the conventions of divine love, and baroque crucifixion. Poetry could serve as heightened recollection. Watts's disadvantage, which Newton did not share, was the sedate prosperity of Independent burghers, which would seem to have called for the deflection of the simple Gospel, of the Beatitudes, for example, into less direct expressions, including a contempt for mundane affairs that purified the heart without compromising the life-style.

Wesley had provided an alternative model, which suited the experience of charismatic enthusiasm. He instructed his singers in the rise and fall of religious feelings, which were regarded as both spurs to and evidence of faith. Wesley's focus on the individual heart marked a turning away from the visual stimulation of Watts, an indication that the singers' response was not quite as trustworthy as it had been and needed to be guided with a firmer hand. The exemplary sensibility of the hymn persona provided a means for leading response in the desired direction. Wesley's model may have struck Newton as insufficiently edifying. Moreover, Newton's Calvinist convictions were fundamentally incompatible with the Methodist dogmas that underlay the method. (Certainly Wesley's almost exclusive focus on the individual heart was not to Newton's taste.) Newton's hymns show the total rejection of both Watts's kind of otherworldliness and Wesley's interiorization of faith.

Newton's successful hymns, even his successful stanzas, are, first of all, those in which he trusts his singers to understand. This attitude is a necessary prerequisite to poetry: the resources of figurative language, however simple, and the conciseness of expression depend upon it. In his trusting hymns, it is significant that the exemplary ring of the verses is muted and we find none of Wesley's strained recitation of ideal response. The poet would seem to be truly one with the singers—although of course instruction is still a vital part of these hymns. Newton's advantages are his compassionate understanding, which allows this unprecedented identification with his people, expressing itself in strong, familiar imagery, and his prophetic vision of the coherence of all experience as the manifestation of God's purpose.

Newton's excellences hinted at a new age of hymnody. Both his charitable interest in common human affairs and his integrating vision of the providential meaning of life implied the irrelevance of that dualism which splits the realms of spirit and flesh. (Watts had idealized the retreat from gross worldly attachments and had worried about the distraction of the fancy. Wesley had grounded spiritual life in the interior emotional processes of the heart.) Neither asceticism nor intense subjectivity suited Newton or Olney, and the features of his best hymns suggest a new appreciation of life in this world *as* life in the Spirit. This integration signaled both a return to an earlier day of belief, unchallenged by the secular Enlightenment, particularly to the dynamic Calvinism of the Puritans, and the transition to a new era in which common humanity would be idealized and the visionary would appreciate history.

Occasionally Newton's hymns fail to educate their singers or to advance their devotional understanding, indicating the lure of purely expressive song, a temptation that recalls the psalms and anticipates a new mode of hymn. This new wave is best observed in Newton's confessional hymns. Traditionally, hymns of exemplary self-examination provided a means of spiritual advancement. Contrition, however abject the singer, yielded, within the same hymn, a devotional advance to confidence and trust. The singers were to be assured of salvation and reconciliation with God—the departure of the New Testament from Psalms. In Newton's confessional hymns we often fail to take this second step. Without such final assurance, without our advance, the hymns become simply expressive. The opportunity for evangelical instruction does not occur because we do not progress beyond exemplary penitence.

This failure to take educational advantage of a hymn is related to the imaginative failure that mars so many of Newton's pedantic hymns, in which the poetic ideas are present—in emblems, images, or associations—but do not develop. The traditional combination of lesson and poetry, as designed by Watts, had apparently ceased to be effective. Instruction and poetry repelled each other. The new poetry spoke eloquently for the poet and singer as one and could teach and refine devotion in a quiet exemplary fashion. Instructive hymns did not even attempt to transcend versification.

❧ V ❧

William Cowper:
Exemplary Tradition
& the Loss of Control

Master Craftsman

William Cowper was considered a "maniacal Calvinist" by Lord Byron and a "poet of the fields" by John Clare, a difference of opinion that suggests the complex diversity of Cowper's large poetic oeuvre. Lines written during a period of tormented insanity, a poem like *The Castaway*, expressing extreme despair of Calvinist election, and poetic accounts of Wordsworthian walks in the countryside find their places among pleasant occasional, satiric, and moral poems perfectly unextraordinary in tenor and expression. Given this variety, the relationship of Cowper's sixty-seven *Olney Hymns* to his later and more famous work is difficult to determine. Understanding of the connection, however, seems to require a grasp of the conventions of hymn writing as they had developed during the preceding decades, particularly as the use of biblical material, the lessons in doctrine, the exemplary devotional attitudes, and the visual and dramatic appeal of the best hymns of the tradition are all evident in Cowper's work.

Cowper's idiosyncrasies, his deviations from the norms of hymn writing despite the master craftsman's understanding of genre discipline, reveal much about the hymn in relation to the more subjective religious lyric. It was not a historical fluke that the English hymn flowered in the great age of public poetry, of "enlightenment," in which truly private terrors and visions were generally kept from view. Nor is it surprising that the resurgence of the lyric impetus was incompatible with the traditional hymn. Didactic purpose filters and directs the expression of strong feelings in the standard hymns of both Cowper and his forebears, a hallmark not of the romantic era but of sensibility.

Gilbert Thomas, Cowper's early biographer, considered his hymns to be too deeply individual for congregational use, *"poems* of personal doubt and conflict rather than *songs* of faith and assurance."[1] Two assumptions lay behind Thomas's judgment: that hymns should be confident, not admitting doubt or hesitation, and that they are properly communal rather than personal in their orientation. When Cowper's achievements and failings are studied with an awareness of the hymn's history, both assumptions must be modified. We have noted that the hymns of Watts, Wesley, and Newton, following the psalms and German models, treated "doubt and conflict" as much as they sang of "faith and assurance." We have seen in the work of these men as well that apparently autobiographical hymns select experience of broad relevance. Watts's insight into common devotional feelings, Wesley's recollection of his conversion, Newton's exceptional sin and his life at sea—all were refined and revised for popular use.

Cowper was familiar with the work of his predecessors and with the standard deployment of personal material. The Olney setting exercised a further control; he wrote with Newton's people in mind. Both the discipline of the genre and of the audience suited a poet who was apparently comfortable with the restrictions of convention. Throughout his life he accepted writing assignments, a creative control that seems not to have interfered with his need to express himself. In his many translations he was held to the subject and tone of the original text. His insanity and his romantic descriptive inclination are best viewed in this context, certainly.

Even when we modify our expectations of hymn confidence and impersonality bearing in mind the work of Cowper's predecessors, we must still cope with the variety signaled by the radically different impressions of Byron and Clare, which is reflected in the hymns. Many are unexceptionally conventional in their exemplary confidence and generalization of personal experience, distinguishable only by their author's skill. Others are models of devotional propriety except for one stanza, often the last, where doubt creeps in or certain powerful images lead the poet astray. Then there are the "terrible hymns," expressing what appears to be a highly idiosyncratic vision of the mystic's dark night of the soul—or sheer personal terror. Each group has its lessons for us in our attempt to define the hymn as genre. All of the groups are determined by Cowper's understanding of hymn purpose.

Cowper's dogmatic hymns provide the expected lessons in doctrine, distinguishing themselves only by their workmanship, the obvious skill of the true professional. In hymn LXIII, "Not of Works," the lesson is the justification by faith alone. The extended stanzas, the use of personification, and the quantity of suggestion in each stanza indicate the full potential of hymn poetry:

> 1   Grace, triumphant in the throne,
>   Scorns a rival, reigns alone;
>   Come and bow beneath her sway,
>   Cast your idol works away.
>   Works of man, when made his plea,
>   Never shall accepted be;
>   Fruits of pride (vain-glorious worm!)
>   Are the best he can perform.
>
> 2   Self, the god his soul adores,
>   Influences all his powers:
>   Jesus is a slighted name,
>   Self-advancement all his aim;
>   But when God the Judge shall come,
>   To pronounce the final doom,
>   Then for rocks and hills to hide
>   All his works and all his pride![2]

The majestic female personification of Grace, before whom we are to bow, contrasts with the false worship of "idol" works, an imaginative and proper central metaphor. The threat of damnation is conveyed in the worm of the second stanza, seeking refuge in the rocks and hills. The metaphor of worldly influence and advancement is nicely integrated.

In the third stanza Cowper uses direct discourse skillfully as he summarizes and answers the argument of righteous pride:

> 3   Still the boasting heart replies,
>   What! the worthy and the wise,
>   Friends to temperance and peace,
>   Have not these a righteousness?

> Banish every vain pretence
> Built on human excellence;
> Perish everything in man,
> But the grace that never can.

The hymn requirements of dramatic entertainment and devotional lesson are both met. The long stanzas and density of poetic thought in such a hymn would presumably be more troublesome for its Olney singers than any subjective indulgence or expression of that "primitive fear" which is supposed typical of Cowper's work.

In Cowper's hymn on the nature of Jesus the carefully wrought theological explanation concludes with another formulation of exemplary confidence:

> 5 A cheerful confidence I feel,
>   My well placed hopes with joy I see;
>   My bosom glows with heavenly zeal,
>   To worship him who died for me.

> 6 As man, he pities my complaint,
>   His power and truth are all divine;
>   He will not fail, he cannot faint,
>   Salvation's sure, and must be mine. [XXV]

The personal-exemplary focus particularly characteristic of Wesley, is seen in "I feel," "my bosom glows," and the death "for me." The model conviction is reinforced by the last stanza, which reviews the nature of Jesus both as man, capable of human pity, and as unfailing and unfainting God. Our own complaining, failing, and fainting are only suggested in contrast. Certainly the poetry of the hymn was improved by Cowper's ability to sustain his thought through a coherent whole.

The complexity of address seen in "Pleading for and with Youth" (XXIII), written for the community of the elect, shows Cowper confronting the challenge of multiple hymn requirements familiar from Wesley and Newton hymns. No evidence of Cowper's extreme fear of exclusion from the chosen ranks is evident. The first stanza reviews the high drama of sin, the sinner, and the Lord. The second stanza frames the first as an account to the Lord of the message that the faithful are constantly impressing upon the young, coupling it with a prayer that continues to stanza 3. The fourth and fifth stanzas address the young people themselves:

> We feel for your unhappy state,
>   (May you regard it too,)
> And would awhile ourselves forget
>   To pour out prayer for you.
>
> We see, though you perceive it not,
>   The approaching awful doom;
> O tremble at the solemn thought,
>   And flee the wrath to come!

In the final stanza the Savior is implored to enjoin the personified "new-born year" to alert everybody to the imminence of God's coming:

> Dear Saviour, let this new-born year
>   Spread an alarm abroad;
> And cry in every careless ear,
>   "Prepare to meet thy God!"

Cowper's success in holding together the complex of address shifts is yet another testimonial to his ability as a hymn writer.

Cowper's strictly conventional hymns present a large bulk of doctrine and exemplary opinion. In these, he speaks from within the ranks of the beleaguered elect (XIV), explaining the relevance of Old Testament experience and teaching correct attitudes toward it (XX). He contrives impressive educational tableaux of the Christian glorified (LI), of the radiant truth of Scripture (XXX), of the easy life of sanctity and grace (L). Subjective response that is common to all Christians is controlled and directed by devotional purpose. Cowper's craftsmanship shows in his employment of direct discourse, the unobtrusive incorporation of Bible verse, and his skillful design of hymns complicated by shifting address. The most distinctive feature of these hymns is simply a credit to Cowper's excellence, as we are encouraged to dwell on a particular image or idea as pleasing and interesting.

Cowper's descriptive skill and imaginative power were such that they often overcharged their hymn vehicle. In the hymns of Watts, we noted that physical detail and clarity of image, whether depicting

violence, pain and death, divine love, or transcendent glory, seemed
intended to jolt the singers into spiritual awareness, bridging by
artistic means the chasm separating man and God. Cowper misses this
effect, and his interest in visualization as often as not leads him astray.
His images are often distracting; Watts might have called them an
indulgence in fancy. The first of Cowper's hymns illustrates this
distraction as symbols laden with traditional religious associations
fuse into a pastoral emblem that is not particularly to the point:

> Oh! for a closer walk with God,
>   A calm and heavenly frame;
> A light to shine upon the road
>   That leads me to the Lamb!

The proximity of "Lamb" to "walk," "light," and "road," each symbolic in itself, results in an earthly rural picture of a country walk,
impinging strangely on the central idea of the hymn.

In hymn XLI, the biblical "roe," panting for "the living stream," is
affected by the closeness of the realistic detail of summer flies:

> 2   The favor'd souls who know
>   What glories shine in him,
>   Pant for his presence as the roe
>   Pants for the living stream!

> 3   What trifles tease me now!
>   They swarm like summer flies,
>   They cleave to everything I do,
>   And swim before my eyes.

The vivid picture of a hot, thirsty deer, bothered by flies, preempts the
stanzas.

When Cowper uses the favorite image of human nature as worm,
the singer becomes "thy rebellious worm" or "vain-glorious worm."
The same visual power, noted above, tends to interfere, resulting in a
grotesquerie quite different from that of Watts. In hymn V, for
example, the vileness of the worm jostles the proud heroism of the
Christian:

> Now, Lord, thy feeble worm prepare!
>   For strife with earth and hell begins;
> Confirm and gird me for the war,
>   They hate the soul that hates his sins. [St. 5]

We are presented with the image of an armed worm.

Hymn LI opens with a reminder of the absolute fallen weakness of the singer:

> I was a grovelling creature once,
>   And basely cleaved to earth;
> I wanted spirit to renounce
>   The clod that gave me birth.

In the following stanzas, the wormlike creature is transformed by God and enjoys a new blessedness:

> But God has breath'd upon a worm,
>   And sent me, from above,
> Wings such as clothe an angel's form,
>   The wings of joy and love.

> With these to Pisgah's top I fly,
>   And there delighted stand,
> To view beneath a shining sky
>   The spacious promised land.

We envision a winged worm. The occasional incongruity of Cowper's pictures suggests his failure to control the imaginative power he possessed. Certainly these pictures distinguish themselves from Watts's carefully ordered tableaux.[3]

Watts's visualizing power was most disturbing in his Crucifixion hymns, which detailed suffering and gore, and in his sacramental hymns, with their powerful suggestions of bloody wine and the flesh of the host. Wesley generally treated the Crucifixion in quite a different manner, inspiring love, admiration, and pity rather than awe-filled terror and accordingly focusing more clearly on the feelings of the singers than on the vision of Calvary. When he wrote of the Crucifixion, Cowper employed both Watts's and Wesley's models. His most powerful Crucifixion hymn, which has spawned a miracle literature of its own, begins with a perfectly coherent tableau, designed, like those of Watts, to enforce certain truth on the singer-spectator:

> 1   There is a fountain fill'd with blood
>   Drawn from Emmanuel's veins;
>   And sinners, plunged beneath that flood,
>   Lose all their guilty stains.
>
> 2   The dying thief rejoiced to see
>   That fountain in his day;
>   And there have I, as vile as he,
>   Wash'd all my sins away.
>
> 3   Dear dying Lamb, thy precious blood
>   Shall never lose its power,
>   Till all the ransom'd church of God
>   Be saved to sin no more. [XV]

The thief's view of the bloody fountain affirms its real, visible nature, while the personal witness of the next two lines projects the vision through history. By the third stanza, the singers have been prepared to address the "dying Lamb," only somewhat oddly informing him that the sacrifice will be effective until the last day.

In the next stanzas, the continued effect of the vision of redemption is assured, but the focus has changed, with the model, to the song itself, which stands at once for Cowper's craft and for the voices of the congregation: we are now singing in Wesley's manner:

> 4   E'er since, by faith, I saw the stream
>   Thy flowing wounds supply,
>   Redeeming love has been my theme,
>   And shall be till I die.
>
> 5   Then in a nobler, sweeter song,
>   I'll sing thy power to save;
>   When this poor lisping stammering tongue
>   Lies silent in the grave.
>
> 6   Lord, I believe thou hast prepared
>   (Unworthy though I be)
>   For me a blood-bought free reward,
>   A golden harp for me!
>
> 7   'Tis strung, and tuned, for endless years,
>   And form'd by power divine,

> To sound in God the Father's ears
>   No other name but thine.

This turn from the vision to the viewer and the subject of song suggests the inadequacy for Cowper of the simple dramatic approach. The song itself is more useful as central theme, and the singer's preoccupation with it now, until death, and after becomes the point. The new focus is the vision of an angelic harp and unceasing song.[4]

Cowper's difficulty in sustaining the splendid picture of his opening three stanzas is hardly surprising if we recall the different poetic and religious world of Watts (and Gerhardt), for whom the vision of the passion was all-sufficient. Visualization overcame the only threat to devotion, namely mundane distraction, and Watts had only to conjure the scene in careful detail. Devotional response for Cowper, as for Wesley, was more subjective, more a function of the individual sensibility.

This explanation of Cowper's difference is sustained by his other Crucifixion hymns, in which the Crucifixion is presented not as particularly sacramental but rather as a supreme lesson in the sort of suffering all believers face in this life:

> The Saviour, what a noble flame
>   Was kindled in his breast,
> When hasting to Jerusalem,
>   He march'd before the rest!
>
> Good-will to men and zeal for God
>   His every thought engross;
> He longs to be baptized with blood,
>   He pants to reach the cross!
>
> With all his sufferings full in view,
>   And woes to us unknown,
> Forth to the task his spirit flew;
>   'Twas love that urged him on.
>
> Lord, we return thee what we can:
>   Our hearts shall sound abroad
> Salvation to the dying Man,
>   And to the rising God!
>
> And while thy bleeding glories here
>   Engage our wondering eyes,

> We learn our lighter cross to bear,
> And hasten to the skies. [XXVIII]

The first three stanzas provide an account of Jesus' innermost feelings on the way to Calvary. The imagery of blood sacrifice is restrained, while the exemplary nobility, zeal, and longing of the Savior are enumerated. The explicit lesson of the last stanza is that we learn from the Crucifixion to bear our own crosses, an exemplary interpretation of Calvary that would seem to clash with the little tableau of the bleeding glories.[5]

The same understanding of the lighter cross pervades the "Prayer for Patience":

> 1   Lord, who hast suffer'd all for me,
>   My peace and pardon to procure,
>   The lighter cross I bear for thee,
>   Help me with patience to endure.

Cowper suggests that the greatest value of Jesus' suffering is that it allowed him to understand and succor humanity in its suffering. After three biblical references (recalling the burning bush as an emblem of angry noise, the abjection of Joshua, and the sins of Babylon), the image of one's own crucifixion returns:

> 5   Ah! were I buffeted all day,
>   Mock'd, crown'd with thorns, and spit upon;
>   I yet should have no right to say,
>   My great distress is mine alone.
>
> 6   Let me not angrily declare
>   No pain was ever sharp like mine;
>   Nor murmur at the cross I bear,
>   But rather weep, remembering thine. [XLIII]

The Crucifixion silences our carping complaints before the Lord.

When Cowper wrote of the sacrament of Communion, he provided a perfect illustration of both his synthesis of traditional items and his own unique contribution. The opening two stanzas of "Welcome to the Table" (XXVII) are strongly reminiscent of Watts:

> This is the feast of heavenly wine
> And God invites to sup;

> The juices of the living vine
>   Were press'd to fill the cup.
>
> Oh! bless the Saviour, ye that eat,
>   With royal dainties fed;
> Not heaven affords a costlier treat,
>   For Jesus is the bread.

The emblematic appeal and the metaphysical details hark back to the standard work of Watts, although the grotesque potential is not exploited (both blood pouring and flesh eating are circumvented). The next two stanzas recall the revival cry of Wesley:

> The vile, the lost, he calls to them,
>   Ye trembling souls appear!
> The righteous in their own esteem
>   Have no acceptance here.
>
> Approach, ye poor, nor dare refuse
>   The banquet spread for you;
> Dear Saviour, this is welcome news,
>   Then I may venture too.

The evangelical call to sinners is modified in line with Cowper's Calvinism, even with his private worries. That the threat of nonacceptance at the Lord's table hangs over the heads of all who regard themselves as righteous is perfectly orthodox, but Cowper implies in stanza 3 that sinners are vile, lost, and trembling. Wesley's confidence is absent as we worry whether we have suffered enough and have humbled ourselves enough to meet the qualifications for entrance. In the following stanza, the poor are ordered to attend; they dare not refuse. Fear, not joy, is the motive force.

The many shifts of address in this hymn indicate the complex task undertaken. We begin with exposition, proceed to an appeal to the communicants to bless the Savior, then hear the Lord explain who is and who is not welcome, then answer the Lord. In the last stanza, the singers hope for acceptance:

> If guilt and sin afford a plea,
>   And may obtain a place,

> Surely the Lord will welcome me,
> And I shall see his face!

In the end, the "Welcome to the Table" is conditional at best. As we look back, the invitation to the feast loses much of its appeal; the mandate to "bless the Saviour, ye that eat," is not so clear. The initial vision is distorted by the last stanza, with its less substantial hope that indeed the singer "shall see his face." This final complication is characteristic of many of Cowper's hymns.

It is tempting to see in Cowper's interpretation of the Crucifixion and of the sacrament manifestations of personal idiosyncrasy, fears and doubts incompatible with hymn purpose. The model suffering of the crucified Lord and the fear of exclusion from the table of the Host would seem to betray Cowper's private vision. These seeming idiosyncrasies are more usefully set in relation to the revival tradition. In Wesley's hymns, one's own feelings became a means to spiritual understanding. Longing, suffering, and misery all contributed to conversion. The Spirit spoke in one's own sighs. Watts's method had been different to the extent that religious truth had a more external, independent, objective existence. Newton's best hymns, similarly, obtain their power from the objectivity with which he viewed the religious integrity of history. Like Wesley's, Cowper's devotional ground, the foundation of response, was subjective experience. The vital importance of each Christian's personal suffering to his or her appreciation of the suffering of Christ on the cross and the real importance of self-accusation and even despair for acceptance by the Lord at the Communion table thus become necessary parts of any hymn about either the Crucifixion or the sacrament.

In this light, self-examination is transformed. Introspective review of one's sins is certainly an orthodox Christian duty, particularly recommended by Pietist tradition. The evangelical revival, with its emphasis on charismatic conversion, had radically modified self-examination, both its means and its ends. Sentiments, in the pure sense, became the primary field of devotional exercise. Cowper was as much in this tradition as he was a Calvinist, and the introspection is reflected in both his faith and his poetry. The Crucifixion as lesson in suffering, the self-consciousness of song, the constructive role of despair as preliminary to revelation, all imply the primacy of emotional response. "The Contrite Heart" (IX) is an exemplary self-

examination that demonstrates the difference between standard confession and the evangelical-charismatic study of one's own devotional sensibility:

> The Lord will happiness divine
>   On contrite hearts bestow;
> Then tell me, gracious God, is mine
>   A contrite heart or no?
>
> I hear, but seem to hear in vain,
>   Insensible as steel;
> If aught is felt, 'tis only pain
>   To find I cannot feel.
>
> I sometimes think myself inclined
>   To love thee, if I could;
> But often feel another mind,
>   Averse to all that's good.
>
> My best desires are faint and few,
>   I fain would strive for more;
> But when I cry, "My strength renew,"
>   Seem weaker than before.
>
> Thy saints are comforted, I know,
>   And love thy house of prayer;
> I therefore go where others go,
>   But find no comfort there.
>
> O make this heart rejoice or ache;
>   Decide this doubt for me;
> And if it be not broken, break,
>   And heal it if it be.

The singer asks neither faith nor forgiveness. Rather, he or she begs
for intensified feelings, to be moved, to feel love and desire. The two
emotions that powered Wesley's hymns, longing and ecstasy, by
failing to materialize create a spiritual vacuum akin to catatonia. At no
point in this hymn is the objective matter of faith presented. We are
left not with personal confession but rather with an *exemplary* probing
of Christian sensibility. Such a self-study depends for its legitimacy on
the premise that heartbreak and healing, aching and rejoicing, are the
only true devotional experiences.

Cowper's Private Vision

The hymn consideration of song to which Cowper turned after the
great fountain of blood reflects Cowper's view of himself as poet. Of
course, the communal design of hymns can successfully mask this
personal element, like so many others, but we are particularly encouraged to consider Cowper's own problems as they may or may not
intrude when he writes of words and faith. In hymn LIX, "A Living
and a Dead Faith," the ultimate inadequacy of fluent speech is
explained, concluding:

> 5   Easy, indeed, it were to reach
>   A mansion in the courts above,
>   If swelling words and fluent speech
>   Might serve, instead of faith and love.
>
> 6   But none shall gain the blissful place,
>   Or God's unclouded glory see,
>   Who talks of free and sovereign grace,
>   Unless that grace has made him free!

The fluency, not of the Olney singers, but of the poet, would seem to
be the issue. While the irrelevance of words to salvation suggests
Cowper's own problems as a believer and the failure of exemplary
confidence that characterizes his fearful hymns, for the singers, at
Olney or elsewhere, the hymn is presumably reassuring to the inar-
ticulate parishioner. Cowper was not as easily led astray as his collaborator was.

It would often appear that the poetry of the hymns itself betrayed
William Cowper into idiosyncratic expression. While his unusual
measure of skill enabled him to exploit the visual and dramatic
possibilities of the genre, the resulting picture frequently seems to tell
more than it ought to. In a "Prayer for Children" (XXIV), the
standard communal voice of the faithful, an Old Testament reference
to the slaughter of the firstborn of Egypt, and a lesson in the need for
Christian education of the young yield a terrifying picture of the
dreadful danger of damnation that hangs over the children:

> Lord, we tremble, for we know
> How the fierce malicious foe,
> Wheeling round his watchful flight,

> Keeps them ever in his sight:
> Spread thy pinions, King of kings!
> Hide them safe beneath thy wings;
> Lest the ravenous bird of prey
> Stoop, and bear the brood away. [St. 3]

The unredeemed terror of this last stanza is a world away from comforting pictures of Jesus surrounded by little ones. With a poet's descriptive power, Cowper has captured the nightmarish fear of a rapacious Satan so successfully as to suggest the inadequacy of the wings of God.

Cowper's vivid depiction of hell, like his vision of the bird Satan, is overly powerful:

> 1   My soul is sad, and much dismay'd,
>   See, Lord, what legions of my foes,
>   With fierce Apollyon at their head,
>   My heavenly pilgrimage oppose!
>
> 2   See, from the ever-burning lake
>   How like a smoky cloud they rise!
>   With horrid blasts my soul they shake,
>   With storms of blasphemies and lies.
>
> 3   Their fiery arrows reach the mark,
>   My throbbing heart with anguish tear;
>   Each lights upon a kindred spark,
>   And finds abundant fuel there.

The singer-poet, the "I" of the hymn, stands in the middle of Milton's hell. Cowper admirably conveys the sensation of damnation along with the lesson of our evil flammability. The language of the prayed for consolation does not balance the intensity of pain and despair. Indeed, the violence of damnation tinges the language of the righteous response that follows:

> 4   I hate the thought that wrongs the Lord;
>   Oh! I would drive it from my breast,
>   With thy own sharp two-edged sword,
>   Far as the east is from the west.
>
> 5   Come, then, and chase the cruel host,
>   Heal the deep wounds I have received!

> Nor let the powers of darkness boast,
>   That I am foil'd, and thou art grieved! [XXXIX]

Rather than, for example, the language of divine love, our faith is cast as *hatred* of certain thoughts that *wrong* the Lord, *driving out* our thoughts with a *sharp sword*. Any comfort in the Lord's healing is overpowered by negative violence, suggestions of unanesthetized psychic surgery, a battlefield between the temples, and the threat of failure and of divine grief.

Cowper's descriptive intensity and his deployment of imagery tend to highlight whatever is aberrant in his cast of mind. His intentions and methods may be orthodox, but the stress falls on the satanic bird or on the firsthand torments of hell, the forces behind evil and suffering being more real to Cowper's imagination than any comforting joys.

In this context, it is useful to recollect Watts's hymn on the ineffable mystery of God. Despite our blindness and the indescribability of heaven, we were shown a heavenly tableau of perfect joy. Cowper's well-known hymn "Light Shining out of Darkness" also attempts the explanation of divine mystery, but, significantly, it is the mystery of apparent evil in a world of God's design; the train of images only complicates the quandary:

> God moves in a mysterious way
>   His wonders to perform;
> He plants his footsteps in the sea
>   And rides upon the storm.
>
> Deep in unfathomable mines
>   Of never-failing skill,
> He treasures up his bright designs,
>   And works his sovereign will.

The enormous, magnificent, Neptune-like god of the first stanza, working his will in sea and storm, is hardly comforting. It is followed in the second stanza by an image of Vulcan, the subterranean crafts-man, not of the loving Father. This double pagan vision introduces four stanzas of instruction in confidence, each one undermined by its own imagery, as our fear of storms, the familiar displeasure of

Providence, the bitterness of life, and its inexplicable vanity are all asked to prove God's hidden beneficence, his kindly purpose:

> Ye fearful saints, fresh courage take,
>   The clouds ye so much dread
> Are big with mercy, and shall break
>   In blessings on your head.
>
> Judge not the Lord by feeble sense,
>   But trust him for his grace:
> Behind a frowning providence
>   He hides a smiling face.
>
> His purposes will ripen fast,
>   Unfolding every hour;
> The bud may have a bitter taste,
>   But sweet will be the flower.
>
> Blind unbelief is sure to err,
>   And scan his work in vain:
> God is his own interpreter,
>   And he will make it plain. [LXVIII]

Even the faithful cannot *see* and must trust that the merciful blessings really are hidden in the dreadful clouds, that gracious smiles are there behind frowning providence, that the sweet flowering of bitter buds will occur. Cowper's descriptive power animates the visible, well-known unpleasantness. The invisible matter of faith is less substantial, almost inaccessible for poetic representation. The weight of the hymn rests on life's cruelty, God's nasty existential masquerade.

Schooled by Watts in hymn design, we expect initial ambivalence, doubt, or hesitation in a hymn as the common understanding is engaged, to be followed by resolution of doubt or clarification of ambivalence. In many of Cowper's hymns, either the doubt is left intact or we proceed, in an impractical reversal, from faith to doubt, as he becomes more and more deeply involved in his explication of devotional difficulty.[6]

The storm was a favorite Cowper image of personal distress, divine fury, and evil force. In hymn XXXVII, Christian life is described as a nightmare sea voyage, in which the words of the psalmist, the fear of the disciples in their boat, and perhaps Newton's

sea stories converge. The hymn attempts to strike exemplary attitudes
but collapses in terror:

> The billows swell, the winds are high,
> Clouds overcast my wintry sky;
> Out of the depths to thee I call,—
> My fears are great, my strength is small.
>
> O Lord, the pilot's part perform,
> And guard and guide me through the storm,
> Defend me from each threatening ill,
> Control the waves,—say, "Peace be still."
>
> Amidst the roaring of the sea,
> My soul still hangs her hope on thee;
> Thy constant love, thy faithful care,
> Is all that saves me from despair.
>
> Dangers of every shape and name
> Attend the followers of the Lamb,
> Who leave the world's deceitful shore,
> And leave it to return no more.
>
> Though tempest-toss'd and half a wreck,
> My Saviour through the floods I seek;
> Let neither winds nor stormy main
> Force back my shatter'd bark again.

The power of the storm and the sailor's fear and weakness are vivid,
while the proffered hope and consolation are diffused. The storm is a
present, active danger, while the Lord's guidance and defense are
requested, not assured. The soul's hope, hung on the constant love
and faithful care of the Lord, is metaphorically outweighed by the
crashing waves. The likelihood of relief is further diminished in stanza
4. Dangers are standard for the faithful, and the terrible sea voyage of
despair is required of the Christian. In the final stanza, the wretched
sailor is in search of his personal salvation, unsure of any guidance,
love, or care at all.

Particular terror derives from the shifting interpretation of the
central image of this hymn. The suffering at sea is at first as natural as
winter and bad weather. In the second stanza, disorientation has

become the problem, then despair. By the fourth stanza, the dangerous voyage has become a cruel requirement. In the last, the voyage is in search of the Savior. As the various storm suggestions are developed, the consolation or exemplary confidence in relief is undermined. The Lord as pilot and defender, who suited the storm as natural, far from exhibiting constant love and faithful care, is elusive.

Cowper's private fear of his own damnation, like his sense of abandonment, fuels many of his hymns, lighting images controlled and directed only with extreme difficulty. In hymn III, the healing power of the Lord is invoked as the singers sing of their common spiritual illness, feeble faith, and faint trust:

> 1 Heal us, Emmanuel, here we are,
>   Waiting to feel thy touch:
>   Deep-wounded souls to thee repair,
>   And, Saviour, we are such.
>
> 2 Our faith is feeble, we confess,
>   We faintly trust thy word;
>   But wilt thou pity us the less?
>   Be that far from thee, Lord!

The image of spiritual illness is not balanced by the healing power of the Lord. Rather than assuring relief, the hymn questions divine pity and hopes for the best.

In the following stanzas, Cowper demonstrates his craftsmanship as he seamlessly incorporates scriptural reference into his verse. But the stress falls on the trembling tears and doubt of the healed boy's father rather than on the fact and promise of healing:

> 3 Remember him who once applied,
>   With trembling for relief;
>   "Lord, I believe," with tears he cried,
>   "O, help my unbelief!"

In the following stanzas, Cowper tries again, turning this time to the woman who touched Jesus' garment:

> 4 She too, who touch'd thee in the press,
>   And healing virtue stole,

> Was answer'd, "Daughter, go in peace,
>   Thy faith hath made thee whole."
>
> 5 Conceal'd amid the gathering throng,
>   She would have shunn'd thy view;
>   And if her faith was firm and strong,
>   Had strong misgivings too.

The faith of the woman is almost regretted as inappropriate, while her unscriptural misgivings are more useful to Cowper's purpose.

The final stanza summarizes the dilemma all too well. We hope and fear; we may not succeed in touching the Lord after all; and then there is the distinct possibility of being sent home deprived even of hope itself:

> 6 Like her, with hopes and fears we come,
>   To touch thee, if we may,
>   Oh! send us not despairing home,
>   Send none unheal'd away.

The confident lesson implied in the title, "I am the Lord that Healeth Thee," has been lost along the way.

When Cowper attempted a hymn in the divine love tradition, he cast his singer in the unsatisfactory role of neglected bride:

> 1 To those who know the Lord I speak,
>   Is my beloved near?
>   The bridegroom of my soul I seek,
>   Oh! when will he appear?

The convention does not suit Cowper's message, and he turns from the bride to a tableau of the glorified Christ:

> 2 Though once a man of grief and shame,
>   Yet now he fills a throne,
>   And bears the greatest, sweetest name,
>   That earth or heaven have known.
>
> 3 Grace flies before, and love attends
>   His steps where'er he goes;
>   Though none can see him but his friends,
>   And they were once his foes.

The invisibility of the Lord to his enemies suggests the bride's true predicament, her miserable alienation. The inexplicable failure of the Lord to shine on all alike is the cause of tremendous evil:

> 4   He speaks—obedient to his call
>   Our warm affections move:
>   Did he but shine alike on all,
>   Then all alike would love.
>
> 5   Then Love in every heart would reign,
>   And war would cease to roar;
>   And cruel and bloodthirsty men
>   Would thirst for blood no more.

That the world is as it is by the unkind will of God is less damaging to this particular hymn, however, than the message of the final stanza, spoken by the abandoned bride:

> 6   Such Jesus is, and such his grace,
>   Oh, may he shine on you!
>   And tell him, when you see his face,
>   I long to see him too. [XXXIII]

The unfavored role of the singer as bride takes us as far as possible from the purpose of the divine love hymns, which was to represent in conventional terms the intimacy between God and humanity.

In Cowper's fearful hymns, we find a combination of Calvinist concern with depravity, election, and divine wrath balanced neither by Watts's "deistic" confidence nor by his alternate confidence in the objective reality of redemption and final reward. Watts's call to otherworldliness, his allegiance to the spiritual realm and distrust of experience of the private sphere are not shared by Cowper, who seems rather to ground his faith, in Wesleyan fashion, in the subjective experience of longing, conversion, and ecstasy. The bridge to God, spun of one's own feelings, could not hold, however, if one retained a Calvinist fear of divine wrath and a conviction of total human depravity. While the longing misery so often seen in Cowper's hymns is reminiscent of Wesley, in Wesley's hymns the pining was inevitably rewarded. The pain differed in kind, as well: it was more general and was rarely poetically fired.

While written to conform to type, Cowper's most interesting hymns nevertheless reflect his personal struggles precisely because the imaginative weight of the poetry falls on the unrelieved images of divine wrath, human suffering, fear, and exclusion. The line is fine between orthodox and nonorthodox hymns because the distinction is a function of the poetry. The continuum begins with unextraordinary suggestions of divine wrath averted (VIII), making praise possible. The next degree is seen in those hymns suggesting that only our humbled misery, at the hand of God, allows salvation by grace (XXXVII). The most terrifying hymns sing of a God of horrible brutality, working his evil will. Across the continuum, we find singers conditioned to abuse, like whipped children or puppies, and the image is always stronger than its counterweight:

> Why should I shrink at thy command,
>   Whose love forbids my fears?
> Or tremble at the gracious hand
>   That wipes away my tears? [XLIV, 2]

While the overt message of the stanza is that we are too quick to fear the hand of God, the shrinking and trembling suggest very real unpleasant past experience.

In the more extreme hymns, Cowper assumes God's brutality and tries to justify such behavior. *Our* suffering, imposed by God, is our means of grace:

> 'Tis my happiness below
>   Not to live without the cross,
> But the Saviour's power to know,
>   Sanctifying every loss;
> Trials must and will befall;
>   But with humble faith to see
> Love inscribed upon them all
>   This is happiness to me.
>
> God in Israel sows the seeds
>   Of affliction, pain, and toil;

These spring up and choke the weeds
   Which would else o'erspread the soil:
Trials make the promise sweet,
   Trials give new life to prayer;
Trials bring me to his feet,
   Lay me low, and keep me there.

Did I meet no trials here,
   No chastisement by the way:
Might I not, with reason, fear
   I should prove a castaway?
Bastards may escape the rod,
   Sunk in earthly, vain delight:
But the true born child of God
   Must not, would not, if he might. [XXXV]

This hymn draws an analogy between God and the father who beats his child. The child is instructed to see the beating as an indication of true paternity, love, and care. His proper place is prostrate at the father's feet. The brutal image is sufficiently dreadful to the modern sensibility that we easily overlook the message: even if we were relieved of affliction, pain, and toil, we would have to seek them out in order to be saved.[7]

Hymn XII employs an alternate analogy, in which the singer is a carthorse that must be whipped to stay on the path. Ephraim's repentance provides the narrative:

1 My God, till I received thy stroke,
    How like a beast was I!
  So unaccustom'd to the yoke,
    So backward to comply.

    . . . .

3 Thy merciful restraint I scorn'd,
    And left the pleasant road;
  Yet turn me, and I shall be turn'd
    Thou art the Lord my God.

    . . . .

6 "My sharp rebuke has laid him low,
    He seeks my face again;

> My pity kindles at his woe,
>   He shall not seek in vain."

It is hardly surprising that Cowper was drawn to translate the work of
Madame Guyon, who wrote

> To lay the soul that loves him low,
>   Becomes the Only-wise:
> To hide beneath a veil of woe
>   The children of the skies.

The doctrinal implications, however, are ill suited to a Protestant
congregational hymn.

"The Shining Light" is one of Cowper's few hymns that lose their
bearing entirely, thereby justifying Thomas's criticism. (We should
not, however, allow an occasional lapse to prejudice our reading of
Cowper's more standard fare.) The horrible despair is unmitigated:

> My former hopes are fled,
>   My terror now begins;
> I feel, alas! that I am dead
>   In trespasses and sins.
>
> Ah, whither shall I fly!
>   I hear the thunder roar;
> The law proclaims destruction nigh,
>   And vengeance at the door.
>
> When I review my ways,
>   I dread impending doom:
> But sure a friendly whisper says,
>   "Flee from the wrath to come."
>
> I see, or think I see,
>   A glimmering from afar;
> A beam of day, that shines for me,
>   To save me from despair.
>
> Forerunner of the sun,
>   It marks the pilgrim's way;
> I'll gaze upon it while I run,
>   And watch the rising day. [XXXII]

The panic is real, fast and noisy. The "friendly whisper" counsels not confidence but flight before God's wrath. The glimmer of hope is distant, if not imaginary. The last stanza, with its elaborate metaphor and continued flight, fails in any way to counter the horror of the preceding four.

Cowper's fearful hymns no doubt betray the poet's disturbed psyche and the unfortunate suitability of certain Calvinist ideas to it. They also suggest—by virtue of their inclusion in the Olney collection—a new tolerance for idiosyncratic expression in congregational hymns, observed as well in certain of Newton's verses. The demarcation between lyrics and hymns, which first blurred when Jacobi, then John Wesley, included Watts's lyrics from the *Horae Lyricae* in their hymn collections, had become almost nonexistent.

It is also evident that Cowper's orthodoxy was not subject to the rigorous examination enjoyed by either Watts or Wesley. His friend and collaborator, Newton, who assembled the Olney collection, was hardly narrow-minded. Moreover, hymns were no longer new and different, subject to scrutiny and liable to be questioned. Neither literary nor theological controls were exercised.

Finally, the personal and professional sense of responsibility of the clergyman presumably played less of a role in Cowper's composition than it had for his predecessors, whose vocations as pastors and preachers had prepared them for their exemplary task. The result was the intrusion of personal and idiosyncratic attitude.

The lyrical transfusion evident in Cowper's hymns, its poetic advantage and occasional distraction, balanced his professional disadvantage. Aside from the skill noted above in Cowper's treatment of dialogue and Bible story, we find his repeated, successful integration of figure and message, symbol and idea, particularly noticeable within the Olney collection in contrast to Newton's awkwardness. Cowper penetrates far more deeply into the nature of what had been for Newton simple, conventional emblems. His theological difficulties seem to have pressed him on, and Cowper's ambivalence about the goodness of God, for example, is reflected in his ambivalence about nature in the hymns. The imagery of storms at sea and the picture of natural beauty and grandeur suggest, alternately, divine wrath and created good. We are returned, within the hymn collection, to the different views of Clare and Byron. As a sometime maniacal Calvinist, Cowper wrote of a fallen natural world or a Creator bent on punishing humankind. As a nature poet, Cowper gave us the country walk and the thirsty deer.

The hymn which often closes the Olney collection demonstrates Cowper's alter ego as a nature poet who in Thomsonian fashion sees the "varied God" manifest in the passing seasons, in dawn and dusk, in created good that is a credit to the goodness of the Maker:

> Winter has a joy for me,
>   While the Saviour's charms I read,
> Lowly, meek, from blemish free,
>   In the snow-drop's pensive head.
>
> Spring returns, and brings along
>   Life-invigorating suns:
> Hark! the turtle's plaintive song
>   Seems to speak his dying groans!
>
> Summer has a thousand charms,
>   All expressive of his worth;
> 'Tis his sun that lights and warms,
>   His the air that cools the earth.
>
> What! has Autumn left to say
>   Nothing of a Saviour's grace?
> Yes, the beams of milder day
>   Tell me of his smiling face.
>
> Light appears with early dawn,
>   While the sun makes haste to rise;
> See his bleeding beauties drawn
>   On the blushes of the skies.
>
> Evening with a silent pace,
>   Slowly moving in the west,
> Shows an emblem of his grace,
>   Points to an eternal rest. [LXVI]

This hymn reminds us of the real value of successfully integrated poetic idea in hymns. We are reminded as well of Watts's similar success, with a difference, and of Newton's frequent failure to make something of the analogies he found all around him.

In the first stanza, Cowper associates winter with infancy, particularly the infant Savior, perfect and unpretentious. The pensive snowdrop's head suggests a threat to innocence, perhaps the weight of sin on purity, and a potential challenge to the "joy" of winter. In the second stanza, treating spring, the infant has yielded to the adult, and the turtle dove of erotic love reflects the sacrificial love of the dying Christ. The combination in four simple lines of the fecundity of spring, sun, sexual longing, and groaning death is an indicator of Cowper's ability to join emblematic idea with descriptive method. The life-powerful spring is also the season of the Crucifixion, and the love longing of the bird reminds us of another pain. The conventional metaphor of divine love has been recast as something that subtly pervades all of our experience. In the third stanza, summer, with all its pleasant attributes, is particularly Christ's time. The subtly threatening suggestion of cooling air, moderating the sun, is only mildly worrisome. The autumn of stanza 4 is all that is left. The question posed in the first two lines, suggesting the exhaustion of the year, seems insufficiently counterbalanced by the affirmation of the next two lines.

Reading these stanzas as poetry, conventionally tracing a human life in the emblematic progression of seasons, autumn signifies sombre mortality ("That time of year thou mayst in me behold"). Quietly running counter to the upbeat prettiness of Jesus mirrored in nature is a train of depressing suggestion. Accordingly, in the last two stanzas Cowper changes his analogy. While they are not absolutely depressing, the seasons have given us decline only. He turns to the progress of day, again presenting natural scenes inspired with religious meaning. The rising sun, the blood-red sky, are familiar emblems, rendered with pleasing descriptive power. The sunset and the coming night are overtly acceptable and serene, canceling in darkness all the flash of day. Under the surface of the poem, Cowper may be grappling with mortal decline ("In me thou see'st the twilight of such day / As after sunset fadeth in the west"), but he controls the imagery very well.

Cowper's self-consciousness as poet, his understanding of precisely what he is doing, is revealed in the reference to emblems in the penultimate line. The entire hymn is an expansion and elaboration of the emblem method: description replaces the emblem drawing as subject for the interpretation. Emblems belong to those who perceive

❧ VI ❧

Conclusion

THIS STUDY of representative hymn writers cannot yield authoritative conclusions about the development of the hymn tradition. Too much material has necessarily been omitted; too many writers and hymns of different and important denominational traditions, particularly the Presbyterians and the Baptists, have been ignored. Moreover, we cannot view the sequence of chapters above as a true progression. To some extent, each writer knew and expanded upon or reacted to the work of his predecessors, but the different historical circumstances and theological principles under which each contributor labored were equally influential, and to a limited degree each writer had to reinvent the hymn as a vehicle for his own message. The essential purpose of the hymn shifted slightly in line with each poet's setting and in accord with the poetic thought of his day. For Watts's Independent congregations, powerful traditional imagery was appropriate; Wesleyan enthusiasm proceeded from and served the spirit of the revival; Newton's prophetic vision suited Olney; and both Cowper's masterful handling of hymn conventions and his idiosyncratic personal hymns reflect his poetical, rather than clerical, vocation. Despite these temporal factors, those hymns that become great poetry—while remaining hymns—achieve a formulation of general Christian relevance, using language that is suggestive of common experience without being idiosyncratic. These hymns demonstrate the normative features of the genre, clarify the purpose and the method of the hymn, and suggest its intriguing relationship to main-line secular literature.

The restraints and restrictions under which the hymn writer labored all derived from the public working of the hymn, from its congregational usefulness. Most of these were anticipated by Watts in his early hymn theory; certainly their place can be seen in the work of all four writers studied here. The first of these restraints is the impersonality of the congregational hymn, particularly apparent in contrast to the devotional lyric. The private convictions of the hymn writer had practically nothing to do with his selection of material, and they colored its presentation only in the most acceptable fashion, as it suited current taste. Watts's progression, his beginning with familiar states of mind, his employment of shocking imagery, his engagement of the passions, all are primarily affective rather than expressive in intent. Wesley's directing of intense passions along evangelically profitable paths, regardless of the sometime artificiality of the charismatic highs and lows, betrays the basically manipulative nature of his hymns—all for the common good and the glory of the Lord. Newton's best hymns proceed from his total identification of himself with his people, for whom he then stands and whom he can then instruct in the basics of the faith, placing them in a world full of providential signs. Cowper's variety, the contrast between his unexceptionably secure hymns and his hymns of despair, best, if inadvertently, suggests the proper suppression of private feeling.

Balancing the characteristic authorial impersonality of the congregational hymn, we find the crucial requirement that hymns touch common experience, engaging their singers' attention and forcing them to recognize the poetry's truth to experience. Not surprisingly for eighteenth-century public poetry, the stress fell on general rather than specific truth, appropriate to the congregational usefulness of the hymns. Affecting hymns required a goodly measure of insight into the mind of the believer. No two hymn writers saw with the same eyes. Watts appealed to the common understanding of divinity, which had apparently been distorted by rational deism, and to his singers' experience of devotional literature and of the psalms. Wesley drew on the familiar human experiences of despair and joy and played out the articulation of stress in naturalistically broken speech, sighs, and groans. Newton's poor hymns illustrate the vital importance of transcending instruction, of not settling for less than poetry. Accordingly, his better work consists precisely of those hymns that assume his singers' grasp of what he was writing about. Cowper's "terrible" hymns demonstrate the uselessness of congregational song that formulates a private vision, expressing no interest in general experience.

The final restriction placed on hymn material and the approach taken to it was that hymns had to be vehicles for correct doctrine and had to teach attitudes that suited the particular sect or movement for which they were designed. As poets working within the confines of particular denominations, subject to constant public review, the hymn writers were limited in much the same fashion as polemicists and political propagandists to orthodox interpretations of truth. Similarly, they were not free, with the possible exception of the layman, Cowper, to write only on favorite themes. These early hymn writers produced collections that covered every imaginable state of devotional mind, a comprehensiveness that complemented their orthodoxy.

It may be argued that only this British literary age, with its understanding of public verse, common truth, and the utility of poetry, could have invented the English hymn as we know it. If the need for impersonality, commonality, and orthodoxy limited the "originality" of the hymn writers, such restraints nevertheless assist the student of hymns by highlighting the writers' distinctly individual understandings of the purpose and function of congregational religious poetry. The different approaches taken by the hymn writers reflect, in turn, the critical debates of the century and one practical side to theological controversy. The conventional restraints also help us understand the introduction of congregational hymns of original composition and their relationship to the metrical psalters. For the hymn writers—as for most modern congregations—the hymns offered something that was missing from the psalms, which we must see as one determinant of the specifications of the hymn type.

The congregational hymn, in all its manifestations, incorporates the common poetic values of its day, most particularly the sought-after balance between specific expression and general experience and the careful alliance of poetic delight and instruction. Neither combination, however theoretically admirable, has ever been free of tension. (Indeed, our postromantic distrust of both general experience and didactic purpose may make it particularly difficult for us to appreciate the heroic effort that was involved.) The suitability of these values to the invention and introduction of the congregational hymn, however, is clear. The positive accomplishments of congregational hymns as poetry may in fact be seen as the result of the interplay between just such a traditional understanding of poetic purpose, of general truth and the instructive duty of literature, and the evangelical challenge to make religion matter. Watts's desire to rouse his singers from indifference, to raise devotional consciousness, Wesley's call to conversion and spiritual fervor, Newton's vision of Christian life in its large providential frame—these inspired courage in the hearts of the poets and led them to experiment with different means of affecting their singers. Under the influence of contemporary moral-psychological theory, traditional mimetic values were transformed by inspirational purpose. The result was the psychological acuity of poetry that began by copying the frequent tempers of the common mind, or turned the singers' attention to the inner voices of the passions and the Lord, or masked its exemplary purpose by the careful reproduction of and reference to everyday experience.

While Watts spoke out, like most critics of his day, against the dangers of the fancy and of boldness, he nevertheless incorporated monologues for Jesus, grotesque tableaux of the Crucifixion, and passionate love scenes in his hymns. The disparity between severe theory and moderate practice, like the contrast between rigorous didacticism and enthusiasm, suggests the true range of hymn possibility. In the context of charismatic religion, imaginative restraint is called for. The particular nature of the dangers he had suspected lurked in the shadows, the overcharging of language and the loss of devotional purpose, became apparent with the wilder hymns of William Cowper, suggesting that the mild restraint of some Augustan aesthetic, some essential distrust of the vagaries of the imagination, was necessary for the development and introduction of this type of poetry. The successful hymns of all of the writers whom we have considered are controlled, both in language and in content, by principles of poetic composition that we regard as native to the eighteenth century.

In our discussion of the entertainment value of the hymns we have been disturbed by our own unsatisfactory terminology for whatever it is that normally balances and moderates the dry pedantry of didactic purpose. Watts wrote of pious pleasure: we have tried "entertainment," "delight," and "enjoyment" to designate the vital component of any hymn that will please its singers. Drama, spectacle, visual clarity, descriptive power, these allowed the poet to enjoin his singers to "See," "Behold," or "Look," to appreciate the work of religious visual art that he had conjured. A different kind of participatory pleasure proceeded from the convincing representation of intense emotion, the sentimental joy of enthusiasm. A third variety set the singer and his or her daily life of struggling faith in a broad, lively, historical frame. Each hymn thus provided a combination of musical, poetical, and visual-dramatic appeal.

Tracing the pious pleasures of hymns, we found that the poet's choice of affective method was determined by an intricate relationship between theological perspective and understanding of poetry. The powerful images traditionally associated with baroque poetry provide an index of the relative importance accorded objective, external, historical, religious material in a particular hymn. In the hymns typical of Watts, the singers were spectators before little dramatic scenes, to which they responded appropriately. The spectacle remained something apart from the singers, however moving or important it may have been. It had objective validity. When Wesley entered his singers into the activity of the hymn, as in his hymn on the prodigal son, he obscured the distinction between modern and New Testament experience, coloring both in the light of charismatic enthusiasm. Accordingly, narrative and descriptive precision became relatively less important in Wesleyan hymns as a new, less objective variety of engagement with the action of the hymn superseded the more traditional kind. Newton seems to have integrated the individual's subjective experience and the larger objective world of religious truth (hence providing "pleasure") by means of a visionary system that transfigured individual, ephemeral experience, raising it to consequential, even mythical, importance. Cowper's hymns show the combination of Watts's powerful clarity (and his Calvinist God) with Wesley's impassioned involvement and subjectively grounded faith.

Two broad categories of educational purpose were served by the congregational hymns. On the one hand, Bible stories and doctrinal positions were explicated and illustrated, a fairly standard type of Christian education, well served by tableaux and scene painting. In these hymns, the believers were informed or reminded of the central matters of faith. Pastoral vocations made the first three hymn writers particularly appropriate creators of educational hymns, which provided an alternative means of religious indoctrination that was less complex and erudite than the traditional sermon and was perhaps more effective for its simplicity. Watts, Wesley, and Newton are noteworthy, even as clergymen, for their commitment to Christian education. Watts wrote textbooks; the Methodists began Sunday schools; Newton could sacrifice most of his hymns to the driest educational purpose imaginable.

The second educational purpose of hymns, their cultivation of devotional sensibility, marked a significant departure from orthodox theological tradition typical of, but not confined to, the evangelical revival. In the hymns of Watts we noted that the worlds of the flesh and the spirit were being reintegrated, that the appropriateness of otherworldliness was being challenged. Watts discreetly suggested that humanity was innately capable of achieving salvation. If its passions were not really legitimate, they could at least serve the end of devotional advancement. Several implications of this new perspective affected the hymn as poetry. We have observed the normative internalization of religious experience in the hymns, a tendency related to seventeenth-century Pietism but seeming to signal, particularly in eighteenth-century context, a retreat before the onslaught of natural religion. Neither Christian action in this world, political or charitable, nor the glories of creation as evidence of God's mastermind, figure in the world view of the hymns we have studied. Hymns reflect, rather, the inward turning and self-examination that locate God's presence in the individual heart. Piety was a passionate affair, and the hymns dealt in passionate exchange.

This attitude implies a trust in human sentiment that fits nicely with contemporary sentimental theories about the improvability of the human lot by means of an appeal to its better feelings. Trust in the heart, as seen in Watts's apologetic, legitimizes the pleasure of literature. It can transform devotional into emotional exercise—as we observed in many of Wesley's hymns. It permits the elevation of the clergyman-poet's ego to a representationally significant position in the visionary scheme of Newton. Cowper's conventional hymns continue in the Watts and Wesley vein, while his extraordinary hymns reject just that hopeful confidence which makes exemplary passion useful. It is not a random coincidence that the hymn writer and the sentimental dramatist both chose an exemplary approach to their material. As we know from the novels of Richardson, the exemplary mode is a natural choice for the writer who would teach his readers a better way to live and who trusts the human heart.

As hymns suggest the modern challenge of finding new religious bearings in a secular age, so their educational methodology suggests the problem of poetry and a pluralistic, popular culture. One major difference between the hymns of Watts, written for a sophisticated and relatively homogeneous community, and those of the revival appeared to be the loss of confidence in the impact of carefully crafted poetry, visually clear, logical, and suggestive, observed in Wesley's hymns. The enthusiastic rush of many of Charles's hymns indicated a need for a new mode that could transport the singers in a rush of convincingly reproduced emotion, teaching them to feel God. New requirements were being made of the language of poetry, a new sort of imitation, not of substantial, perceived reality, but rather of emotional intensity. The failure of traditional poetic means to work the needed transformation is further suggested by Newton's difficulties. In situations in which Watts could have written convincingly and imaginatively, Newton settles for doggerel, the most basic versification. His hymns that become real poetry do so in new terms, adjusted to the limited experience of his singers and expecting only very basic familiarity with the Christian faith. It is difficult to imagine the same congregation of believers appreciating the poetic density of Cowper's more masterful hymns. (We have no evidence that it did or did not.)

With the foregoing conclusions about the purpose and the poetry of hymns in mind, we can return to review the metrical psalms with new insight into their relationship to the hymns. In the first place we recall that the psalms were viewed as predominantly expressive, more suitable for private use. The inspirational and educational purpose assigned the congregational hymn is quite different. When Watts and Wesley attempted to adapt the psalm texts to hymn purpose they faced an impossible challenge, the clash of genres. Second, if Newton's labored Old Testament hymns are any indication, it is evident that, by his day if not earlier, the traditional typological reading of the psalms, centering on the identification of the Christian singer with the people of Israel, was no longer easy and spontaneous, particularly among the unlettered and unchurched masses to whom the evangelical revival attempted to minister. If Newton needed to spell out the relevance of the Old Testament in such great detail, it may be assumed that his people had considerable difficulty understanding psalmody. Hymns tried to be more direct, less dependent on tradition, even the scriptural tradition so essential to classical Protestantism.

Finally, we must remember that neither the Old nor the New Version of Psalms had achieved the timeless grace of the King James Bible and that the New Version of Tate and Brady was particularly seriously flawed as poetry. When we recall, for example, the greater measure of subjectivity apparent in the New Version of Psalms than in the Old, the interiorization of devotion seen not in any Wesleyan passion but rather in the pale diffusion of language, the loss of anthropomorphicity, and the lessened sense of intimate communion with God, we can appreciate the inadequacy of the metrical psalters to meet the challenge at hand. The New Version would seem to reflect the same crisis in faith that yielded the hymns, a loss of spiritual vitality. Unlike the hymns, however, it fails to transcend that loss and settles for a glossy sort of subjectivity, neither overpowering nor immediate.

In the context of these conclusions about the congregational hymns in England, we can also return to the German models and the suggestions of possible influence outlined in chapter 1. The presence in London of hymn-singing Germans, who often discreetly called their songs "psalms," and the similarities between German hymns of the seventeenth century and the new English varieties, suggest that the historical background of the English development includes the sensitivities of the Pietist baroque. The failed objectivity and the general difficulty of faith, which are implied in the New Version of the psalter, the countering of which Watts took as his major challenge, ally the crises of the age to the earlier time. The devotional aesthetic that underlay the hymns of Paul Gerhardt proved useful, and in their sensationalism Watts's (and Cowper's) blood-and-wounds hymns resemble their Pietistic counterparts. Similarly, while the subjectivity of Wesley's hymns may mark a new approach within the English tradition, the model of the Moravian hymns was both appropriate and familiar.

Once we distinguish eighteenth-century hymns from subjective lyrical poetry and come to respect the authority of the verses, hymns provide a means of studying different theological perspectives as they affect the believer's sense of self and the larger world. In other words, the poetic handling of doctrine and the doctrinal influence on poetry provide clues to the understanding of both the poetry and the religion of an age. The attractions of bloody spectacle and divine love in Independent London in the first decade of the eighteenth century suggest the wealth and intricacy of dissenting culture. The sensationalism of many hymns balances the impression of cool reasonableness given by published sermons and works of "divinity." Certainly the momentary compatibility of Protestant baroque, Augustan, and sentimental values, seen in Watts's hymns, renders suspect our view of these as distinct, even mutually exclusive, historical phenomena. The decontrol of sensibility effected by Wesley's rejection of decorous restraint suggests useful perspectives on the nature of enthusiasm and its relation to sensibility. The need for a new style of Christian propaganda for the unlettered masses as it affected the poetic values of the hymn writers, particularly Newton, has implications for the contemporary development of popular literature.

Hymns provide a useful vantage point from which to survey the complex and diverse world of eighteenth-century thought, particularly as they reflect the interrelations among such phenomena as deism, enthusiasm, rationalism, sentimentalism, sensibility, evangelicalism, and romanticism. The hymns also demonstrate a surprising influence of foreign religious writing, Catholic and Protestant, indicated by the influence of Sarbiewski, the Polish Jesuit poet, on Watts, the appeal of the German Pietists and the Moravians for the Wesley brothers, and the similarities of certain of Cowper's ideas to those of Madame Guyon. Such a vital literary subculture, open to unusual foreign influences, must have played its part in the larger literary historical drama of the time. It certainly deserves recognition. When he admired Watts's prose for its efficacious piety, Samuel Johnson complimented those same qualities that distinguish Watts's hymns and that are products of the same literary subculture. When we approve Watts's advocacy of female education or applaud Wesley's acceptance of women preachers (concerning whom Johnson's feelings are well known), we ought to see these as manifestations of a lively tradition, no less important than the more prominent tradition for not being standard.

Historical connections indicated or confirmed by hymn study include the close relationship between seventeenth-century Puritan introspection and eighteenth-century secular sensibility and the essential incompatibility of Calvinism with enthusiasm. The tacit acceptance of certain principles of rational deism, even by dissenters and evangelicals, which limited religious experience to the private sphere, seems especially significant. The basically secular concern of psychology and rational deism were countered by a devotional introversion that is neither Pietistic in the Puritan manner, nor "romantic" in any meaningful sense of the term. These developments conform to our understanding of psychologically (or sentimentally) grounded faith.

While we have not tried to define the literary tradition to which hymns belong, we have noted that the German influence, the religious societies, and the poetry of the metrical psalters have not been seriously considered by literary historians. This oversight has confused students of the century about the place of hymns and the nature of the religion of the age, certainly, but has also led to the neglect of a body of evidence that promises to refine our appreciation of the world view of more "acceptable" genres: satirical prose and verse, novels, Horatian poetry, and serious drama share many presuppositions and literary attitudes conspicuously present in the hymns of the age.

We hope that even if we fail in our efforts to prompt a thorough reevaluation of the importance of hymns in the understanding of eighteenth-century literary history, we may at least lay to rest the widely held theory that eighteenth-century hymns are the first cousins of romantic poetry, sharing the same heartfelt and spontaneous lyrical and popular ancestors. Frederick Gill, to take one example among many, saw the emphasis on nature of the early romantics, and the emphasis on love of the later romantics, as anticipated by the Methodist hymns.[1] In sharp contrast, we have noted how generally nature is neglected in eighteenth-century hymns, even as a standard, deistic manifestation of God's creative achievement, and how unperturbed the hymn writers seem to have been by the thought of the final destruction of all created good. Wesley was notably indifferent to descriptive detail. The passionate abandon of Wesley's hymns is perhaps more interesting as a possible precedent to romantic feeling, but only if we can establish—in the face of considerable evidence to the contrary—that Wesley's hymns, like Shelley's poetry, are fundamentally egotistical. We have maintained that Wesley wrote script for aspiring converts, teaching them to feel or demonstrating proper devotional attitudes. The reader of Shelley's love poetry contemplates a predominately narcissistic emotion, generated by and returning to the poet-subject.

Stylistically, the hymns have seemed to many to anticipate romantic poetry, especially the ballads of Wordsworth and the lyrics of Blake. Gill has noted the resemblance between the poetic principles Wordsworth expounds in his preface to the second edition of the *Lyrical Ballads* and those put forward by John Wesley in his preface to the hymn book of 1779. Wordsworth advocates for poetry "simple and unelaborated expressions" of common people, those arising from "repeated experience and regular feelings." These constitute in Wordsworth's view a "more permanent, and a far more philosophical language, than that which is frequently substituted for it by Poets." This statement seems close to John Wesley's view that the Methodists spoke "common sense," using words only "in a fixed and determinate sense." In their language he found purity, strength, and elegance, combined with "the utmost simplicity and plainness, suited to every capacity." Both Wordsworth and John Wesley, then, stress the importance of simplicity and familiarity of style, as well as the connection between this simplicity and strength of expression. The "permanent" language of Wordsworth is obviously close to the "determinate" one of Wesley, although in Wordsworth its primary aim is lasting poetry, whereas in Wesley it is the reading of "every capacity."

When we turn from the theory to the practice, we find that in many of the poems of the *Lyrical Ballads,* Wordsworth strays far from the language of Cumberland shepherds, and as Coleridge noted, he presents his unique vision in language as complex as the vision, language that becomes a mode of his own self-revelation. Because of their didactic aim and because of the congregational use of their work, the hymn writers on the whole adhere to the standards of simplicity they set for themselves. They gain complexity not through greater sophistication of language and subtlety of meaning but through the echoes and associations given their words from their use in the Bible.

The comparison of hymn style and manner with Blake's poetry is more insistent than the comparison with Wordsworth, and it has been more frequently made. Thomas B. Shepherd, Jacob Bronowski, and Martha England have all noted the influence of Charles Wesley's hymns on the *Songs of Innocence and Experience,* illustrated in the shared diction, stanza form, and rhyme words.[2] The differences are as notable. Unlike the hymn writers, Blake is not limited by sectarian doctrine, and although the false doctrine hymns of Wesley and Newton in some respects resemble the contrary stanzas of the *Songs,* they lack the subtle irony and the complexity that comes from the juxtaposition of two genuinely possible modes of vision. Blake forces the reader into thought, the result of such subtlety and complexity; the hymn writers arrange their singers in devotional attitudes that are irresistible and unmistakable. In his later poems Blake's myths, although heavily influenced by biblical ones, often become private and initially obscure; they are presented in complex, even cryptic language, and the poetic and self-revelatory aim, as in Wordsworth, usually predominates over the public and didactic.

The relationship of Blake's prophet to Newton's or Wesley's preacher seems at first sight close. Blake believed that he was descended from the biblical prophets Isaiah and Ezekiel; he was sure of his election to prophecy and he saw himself renewing the prophetic vision for his generation, much as Newton believed he was revealing God's direct action in his time. There is, however, a difference in conception, and so in effect, between Blake's prophet and Newton's preacher. Something of this difference is suggested in an essay entitled "Blake's *Jerusalem:* The Bard of Sensibility and the Form of Prophecy," by Harold Bloom. Bloom makes a distinction between Blake's prophet and the bard of sensibility that can be extended also to the preacher. According to Bloom, the bard of sensibility is marked by "the terrible double vision of what was and what is, Eternity and the categories of mental bondage, the fallen forms of space and time. . . . Freedom for the prophet means freedom from the detachment of the histrionic mode [in which the poet is both actor and audience]: the prophet retains a sense of himself as actor, but he ceases to be his own audience."[3] Where the preacher of the hymn writers is given a sense of collectivity in his role and in the audience, Blake's prophet is deprived of it. The preacher is exemplary and representative, and his creator both plays the role and watches the playing. Caught in the absolute contrast of humanity and God, the preacher is fixed in both doctrine and posture; the Blakean prophet is not tied to doctrinal absolutes, and his stance is individual and free.

Most of the differences in method between the hymns and romantic poetry are due to different aims. The overwhelming didactic aim of the hymns, both doctrinal and devotional, clearly separates them from the secular poetry of the early nineteenth century. Occasionally, however, when a poet of this period had an overt didactic intention similar to that of the hymn writers, he used some of the elements characteristic of the hymns. For example, when Shelley wrote to instruct the common people and to awaken in them the correct emotional response, he realized that a special style was needed, one "adapted to the lowest comprehension that can read."[4] A body of verse adapted in this way already existed in the hymns and it is not surprising that when Shelley wrote his "Song to the Men of England," he should employ many elements familiar from the hymns, including the dramatic description, the sudden emotional appeal, and the extreme imagery:

1   Men of England, wherefore plough
    For the lords who lay ye low?
    Wherefore weave with toil and care
    The rich robes your tyrants wear?

2   Wherefore feed, and clothe, and save,
    From the cradle to the grave,
    Those ungrateful drones who would
    Drain your sweat—nay, drink your blood?

3   Wherefore, Bees of England, forge
    Many a weapon, chain, and scourge,
    That these stingless drones may spoil
    The forced produce of your toil?

4   Have ye leisure, comfort, calm,
    Shelter, food, love's gentle balm?
    Or what is it ye buy so dear
    With your pain and with your fear?

5   The seed ye sow, another reaps;
    The wealth ye find, another keeps;
    The robes ye weave, another wears;
    The arms ye forge, another bears.

6   Sow seed,—but let no tyrant reap;
    Find wealth,—let no impostor heap;
    Weave robes,—let not the idle wear;
    Forge arms,—in your defence to bear.

7   Shrink to your cellars, holes, and cells;
    In halls ye deck, another dwells.
    Why shake the chains ye wrought? Ye see
    The steel ye tempered glance on ye.

8   With plough and spade, and hoe and loom,
    Trace your grave, and build your tomb,
    And weave your winding-sheet, till fair
    England be your sepulchre.[5]

In this poem, written primarily in the long measure of hymns, the extreme imagery of chains and death and, most obviously, of masters drinking the blood of the workers, resembles the baroque imagery of Watts or Cowper. A reader with any background in hymn singing cannot avoid the Christian sacrificial associations of this blood, and indeed, the image gains force from the many hymns that use it, while the workers gain mythic significance as unwilling Christs forced to sacrifice themselves for their masters' sins and to save them at the price of their own pain.

As in the hymns, so in Shelley's poem, biblical allusions give resonance to the phrases. The line "The seed ye sow, another reaps" gains force from the biblical threat that as we sow, we must reap. Here the threat is not to the evil sowers but to the timid good. The tableau technique of the hymns is employed in stanza 7, where the workers are presented in chains of their own making, menaced by weapons they themselves forged. At the end of the "Song," the consequences of not acting according to the political ideas of the poet resemble in effect Newton's description of false belief.

To see similarities between the "Song" of Shelley and the hymns is not to posit a direct line of influence from the Methodists and evangelicals to Shelley. Rather, it is to suggest that when the aim is public instruction and emotional education, the means chosen at this period to meet such an aim will be similar.

Blake was nearer in time than Shelley to the early hymn writers, and he shares more of their characteristics. Like them, he was steeped in the language and typology of the Old Testament, and the prophetic role is as important in his poetry as it is in the hymns of Newton. As we noted, his aims, and so usually his style and method of presentation, differ from those of the hymn writers. Like Shelley, however, Blake occasionally wrote stanzas that, through their use of hymn elements, catch the flavor of the congregational hymn as it was written in the eighteenth century. The opening poem of *Milton* caught it so successfully that it was arranged for congregational singing in the late nineteenth century by Herbert Parry:

> And did those feet in ancient time.
> Walk upon Englands mountains green:
> And was the holy Lamb of God,
> On Englands pleasant pastures seen!
>
> And did the Countenance Divine,
> Shine forth upon our clouded hills?

And was Jerusalem builded here,
Among these dark Satanic Mills?

Bring me my Bow of burning gold:
Bring me my Arrows of desire:
Bring me my Spear: O clouds unfold!
Bring me my Chariot of fire!

I will not cease from Mental Fight,
Nor shall my Sword sleep in my hand:
Till we have built Jerusalem,
In Englands green & pleasant Land.[6]

In the "I" of this poem, all the people are brought to a mythic level; they take part in the mythic drama of arming themselves and preparing for the fight that is also the building of the new Jerusalem in England and a repetition of the restoring of Jerusalem in Zechariah. The England of Blake is as real as the Olney of Newton, and the Jerusalem established there is both actual and symbolic. Like Olney, England is not reduced by its association with Jerusalem but is magnified and is set in a context of eternity. The English are both the type of the chosen Jews and the chosen people themselves.

In the third stanza the drama resolves itself into a tableau of the Christian girt, like Paul's righteous man in Ephesians or Newton's Christian, with the panoply of the Lord. The attributes of the figure, the arrows of desire and the chariot of fire, weld the erotic and spiritual while at the same time keeping both elements distinct. In much the same way material and symbol come together in the spiritual Jerusalem set firmly in the hills of England that are both green and hellish. As Cowper's lamb grazed on the fields of Buckinghamshire, so Blake's lamb has a "pasture" in the pleasant land of England. Both poets risk the grotesque and gain dramatic tension through the risk.

Blake's poem is in direct speech throughout. Its wondering opening gives place to an ordering of a new existence that brings sureness in much the same way as Watts's "Indescribable" bright abode of the Lord or Newton's Zion City. Although there is only one speaker in the poem, an appearance of dialogue is given by the answering of questions with certainty.

Another poem by Blake employing other techniques of the con-

gregational hymn, especially the specificity of Watts and Newton
and the grotesque transformations of Cowper, is "The fields from
Islington" from *Jerusalem*. In this poem, Blake uses biblical
material in something of the way Newton did, and he gives it
similar specificity. The first few stanzas of this long poem can
illustrate its tone and style, as well as some of its hymnlike
qualities:

> The fields from Islington to Marybone,
> To Primrose Hill and Saint Johns Wood:
>   Were builded over with pillars of gold,
> And there Jerusalems pillars stood.
>
>   Her Little-ones ran on the fields
> The Lamb of God among them seen
>   And fair Jerusalem his Bride:
> Among the little meadows green.
>
>   Pancrass & Kentish-town repose
> Among her golden pillars high:
>   Among her golden arches which
> Shine upon the starry sky.
>
>   The Jews-harp-house & the Green Man;
> The Ponds where Boys to bathe delight:
>   The fields of Cows by Willans farm:
> Shine in Jerusalems pleasant sight.
>
>   She walks upon our meadows green:
> The Lamb of God walks by her side:
>   And every English Child is seen,
> Children of Jesus & his Bride,[7]

As Olney became a biblical city, so London here becomes Jerusalem.
The sudden new perspective on the ordinary resembles the vast
evangelical context of time and space in which Newton set the earthly
community. The tableau technique of Watts is used to present the
little children running in the fields, fields that, like Cowper's, contain
the spiritual and also inescapably physical Lamb of God. In stanza 2
the transformations of images—the Lamb in the pasture runs with the
children and then becomes the bridegroom of Jerusalem—is similar in

effect to the transformations of Cowper's cringing worms into winged warriors.

Other sections of the poem contrast the vast vision of the rich Jerusalem with the "Mortal Worm," which humanity became. Through the drama of the "I," they also direct the exemplary horror of the reader, followed by dramatic commitment to the rebuilding of Jerusalem.

In "Song to the Men of England" and the stanzas from *Milton* and *Jerusalem,* Shelley and Blake have primarily didactic and public aims. Like the evangelical prose of Hervey and the hymns, they appeal directly to the readers, requiring a predetermined political or religious response. They assume a community of interest; the building of Jerusalem and the forging of arms refer both to inner changes and to communal endeavor. The poems bind their special readers together and provide them with a community of feeling and of purpose. They differ from the evangelical hymns only in doctrine.

Louis Benson maintained that the *Olney Hymns* mark a point of transition in English hymnody. They were, he wrote, the last of a group of books bringing evangelical hymnody into the Church of England without severe adaptation.[8] We have related the eighteenth-century dissenting and evangelical hymn to the contrived subjectivity of sentimental literature and the revival movement in its enthusiastic phase. As both declined in the early years of the nineteenth century, so did the evangelical hymn. In its place there grew up an Anglican version of hymn, purged of revival elements and genuinely influenced by contemporary romantic poetry. Most of the major romantic poets occasionally wrote hymns, but none put any creative effort into them.[9] Their own poetry, however, served as inspiration for hymns that became quasi-lyrical expressions of unspecific religious feeling rather than presentations of correct doctrine and devotional reaction. A brief glance at the first notable Anglican hymnbook influenced by nineteenth-century poetry will indicate the difference and will suggest how far hymn writers were moving from Watts's fear of the literary hymn and from Newton's distrust of poetic language.

Reginald Heber's *Hymns, written and adapted to the weekly church service of the year* was published in 1827. The hymns follow the church year rather than the emotional vicissitudes of the Christian life, indicating that they were now included in the service proper. They please and mildly inspire but do not shock and manipulate, and they concentrate not on the Crucifixion of Jesus but on his birth, which becomes a picturesque and touching event, devoid of shadowy Calvinist implications:

> Brightest and best of the sons of the morning!
>   Dawn on our darkness and lend us thine aid!
> Star of the east, the horizon adorning,
>   Guide where our infant Redeemer is laid!
>
> Cold on his cradle the dew-drops are shining,
>   Low lies his head with the beasts of the stall,
> Angels adore him in slumber reclining,
>   Maker and Monarch and Saviour of all![10]

Nature becomes for Heber good and beautiful, something for which to praise God. It yields a moral message in passing:

> I prais'd the Earth, in beauty seen
> With garlands gay of various green;
> I prais'd the Sea whose ample field
> Shone glorious as a silver shield
> And Earth and Ocean seem'd to say
> "Our beauties are but for a day!"[11]

Finally, Heber's hymns minister to the greatness both of God and of humanity, no longer vile and wormlike in the Cowper manner. They must have been especially inspiring to Englishmen in their imperial role, and the hymn "From Greenland's Icy Mountains" set the pattern for many hymns to come:

> From Greenland's icy mountains,
>   From India's coral strand,
> Where Afric's sunny fountains
>   Roll down their golden sand;
> From many an ancient river,
>   From many a palmy plain,
> They call us to deliver
>   Their land from error's chain.[12]

The singers of such hymns are mildly uplifted and edified; they praise a rather distant God, beneficent, impersonal, and imperial, and they wonder at the grandeur and beauty of his works. They learn no doctrine and experience no terror at the vast gulf between the omnipotent God and vile humanity, no ecstasy of conversion, and no transformation of daily affairs into providential signs. Their God will come in splendor in the fullness of time, wending his way through the imperial possessions. He no longer busies himself with the affairs of Olney lace makers or rewards the emotional commitment of his chosen few with a private hiding place.

Notes

CHAPTER ONE

1. John Julian, D.D., ed., *A Dictionary of Hymnology: Setting forth the Origin and History of Christian Hymns of All Ages and Nations*, rev. with supp., 2 vols. (New York: Dover, 1907). Originally published in 1892, the dictionary was reissued, unabridged and unaltered, in 1957.

2. Louis Benson, *The English Hymn: Its Development and Use in Worship* (1915; reprint ed., Richmond, Va.: John Knox, 1962).

3. Eric Routley, *The Music of Christian Hymnody: A Study of the Development of the Hymn Tune since the Reformation, with Special Reference to English Protestantism* (London: Independent Press, 1957), p. 93.

4. *The Hymns of Wesley and Watts: Five Informal Papers* (London: Epworth Press, 1942), p. 14.

5. *The Evangelical Doctrines of Charles Wesley's Hymns* (London: Epworth Press, 1941), p. 86.

6. Martha England and John Sparrow, *Hymns Unbidden: Donne, Herbert, Blake, Emily Dickinson, and the Hymnographers* (New York: New York Public Library, 1966), p. 82.

7. Frederick John Gillman, *The Evolution of the English Hymn: An Historical Survey of the Origins and Development of the Hymns of the Christian Church* (London: George Allen and Unwin, 1927), p. 214.

8. Hoxie Neale Fairchild, *Religious Trends in English Poetry*, 6 vols. (New York: Columbia University Press, 1939–62), vol. 1, *Protestantism and the Cult of Sentiment, 1700–1740*, p. 32.

9. *Congregationalism in England, 1662–1962* (London: Independent Press, 1962), p. 129.

10. "Romanticism and the Hymns of Charles Wesley," *Evangelical Quarterly* 46 (October/December 1974): 202.

11. *Times Literary Supplement*, November 26, 1976, 1491–92.

12. It is undeniable that we have left out hymn writers of stature, including Philip Doddridge and the Baptists. We can make no claim that this study is a history of the eighteenth-century hymn.

13. Benson, to whom we are indebted for the historical material of this section, describes the Lutheran hymns as the lineal successors of the Latin hymns of the Breviary, while the Calvinist psalm was the successor of the old church psalmody, a main feature of the Daily Office *(English Hymn,* p. 24). Edna Parks has provided a detailed examination of the early hymns of the metrical psalters: *The Hymns and Hymn Tunes Found in the English Metrical Psalters* (New York: Coleman-Ross, 1966).

14. Preface to *The Psalms of David Imitated in the Language of the New Testament. And apply'd to the Christian State and Worship* (London: J. Clark, 1719), p. xi.

15. Quoted in Charles S. Phillips, *Hymnody Past and Present* (New York: Macmillan, 1937), p. 171. The fact that scholars have quickly accepted Wesley's highly questionable judgment says more about the changes in the English language than about the poetry of the Old Version. Christopher Dearnley, for example, writes of the "inherent weaknesses of their clumsy paraphrases," in *English Church Music, 1650–1750, in Royal Chapel, Cathedral, and Parish Church* (New York: Oxford University Press, 1970), p. 140.

16. "A Tous Chrestiens: De l'vtilité des Pseaumes" (Anvers, 1563).

17. There is a standard critical refusal, not only among hymnologists, to recognize any German influence on English literature before mid-century. Such an attitude is unreasonable, particularly in the domain of religious literature. Most obviously, the accession of the German Hanoverians meant the influx of Germans into England. Even before George I, however, we find records of German pastors preaching in London, acting as chaplain to Anne's Danish prince consort and, even earlier, influencing the movement of the religious societies at the end of the seventeenth century. See England and Sparrow, *Hymns Unbidden,* p. 38: "Germanic studies in England were nonexistent in 1737 when John Wesley introduced into English the first influence of German hymnody."

18. Martha England discusses this book in England and Sparrow, *Hymns Unbidden* (pp. 31–42). The text is available in facsimile, edited by Frank Baker and George Walton Williams, as *John Wesley's First Hymn Book: A Collection of Psalms and Hymns* (1737; facsimile ed., Charleston: Dalcho Historical Society, 1964).

19. *Psalmodia Germanica; or, The German Psalmody. Translated from the High German. Together with their Proper Tunes, and Thorough Bass,* 3rd ed. (London: J. Haberkorn, 1765).

20. Werner P. Friederich, "Late Renaissance, Baroque or Counter-Reformation?" *Journal of English and Germanic Philology* 46 (January 1947): 135–36. See also Harold B. Segel, *The Baroque Poem: A Comparative Survey* (New York: Dutton, 1974), p. 82.

21. Taken from *A Collection of Hymns, with several Translations from the Hymn-Book of the Moravian Brethren* (1743). James Hutton, a prominent English Moravian, published this collection of acceptable translations.

22. *A Collection of Hymns: Consisting chiefly of Translations from the German,* part 3, 2nd ed. (London, 1749). According to the "advertisement" to this second edition, the hymns of the first had been printed as prose to save money.

23. A copy is in the British Library.

24. As an older man, Watts was in close contact with Frederick Michael Ziegenhagen, chaplain to George II, and he corresponded with Count Zinzendorf, Ziegenhagen's antagonist and leader of the Moravian Brethren. Watts's prose works were translated into German and were used at Halle, the center of the Pietist movement. Philip Doddridge, Watts's protégé and a distinguished hymn writer in his own right, "was the grandson, on his father's side, of one of the ministers ejected under the Commonwealth, and on his mother's side, of a Lutheran pastor who had fled from Bohemia for conscience' sake" (Gillman, *Evolution of the English Hymn,* p. 211).

25. 2nd ed. (London, 1698). See also Richard Kidder, *The Life of the Reverend Anthony Horneck, D.D.,* A Library of Christian Biography, vol. 12 (London: John Mason, 1840). The societies were considered by Escott to be "living cells of psalm and hymn experimentation" (Harry Escott, *Isaac Watts, Hymnographer: A Study of the Beginnings, Development, and Philosophy of the English Hymn* [London: Independent Press, 1962], p. 77). While they cannot be definitely linked to Watts, they were an important influence on the Wesleys and on George Whitefield.

26. John Jacob Rambach, *Memoirs of the Life and Death of the late Reverend Mr. Anthony William Boehm Formerly Chaplain to his Royal Highness Prince George of Denmark, and Minister of the German Chapel at St. James in London Together with A particular Account of his Exemplary Character, and of his Writings,* trans. John Christian Jacobi (London: Richard Ford, 1735). Works of Boehm listed by Rambach include *Pietas Hallensis; or, A public Demonstration of the Foot-steps of a divine Being yet in the World; in an Historical Narration of the Orphan House, and other charitable Institutions at Glancha near Halle,* 8 vols. (1705).

27. It is tempting forthrightly to label these anachronistic elements "baroque." Since the word came into fashion as a literary historical term, however, so many cautions have been issued regarding its misuse that we shall resist the temptation. Perhaps "what appears baroque to many observers may be also medieval or simply universally Christian, such as the paradoxes of the Christian faith, or even generally human, like the fear of death or lust for the other sex" (René Wellek, "The Concept of Baroque in Literary Scholarship," *Journal of Aesthetics and Art Criticism* 5, no. 2 [December 1946]: 94).

28. George Henry Vallins, *The Wesleys and the English Language* (London: Epworth Press, 1957), p. 71.

29. J. Ernest Rattenbury, *The Eucharistic Hymns of John and Charles Wesley* (London: Epworth Press, 1948), p. 110.

30. Marc F. Bertonasco, *Crashaw and the Baroque* (University: University of Alabama Press, 1971), pp. 3–42.

CHAPTER TWO

1. While his treatment of hymns is not particularly reliable, Robert Tudor Jones has provided a comprehensive history of Independency in *Congregationalism in England, 1662–1962* (London: Independent Press, 1962). The Independents were a minority within the dissenting faction who disagreed with the Presbyterian desire for a uniform church government. They were upstanding, conservative, bourgeois Calvinists who were particularly interested in education, as their children had been barred from the universities. Samuel Johnson was criticized for praising a dissenter in his *Life of Watts.* See James H. Leicester, "Dr. Johnson and Isaac Watts," *New Rambler,* 17 (June 1964): 2–10. Harry Escott has written a modern, if somewhat partial, biography of Watts: *Isaac Watts, Hymnographer: A Study of the Beginnings, Development, and Philosophy of the English Hymn* (London: Independent Press, 1962).

2. Preface to the *Horae Lyricae,* p. vi. Citations refer to the "altered and much enlarged" edition of 1709. It is misleading either to identify hymns with these poems or to suggest that the preface is "one of the most significant documents in eighteenth-century literary criticism." See Escott, *Isaac Watts,* p. 61, and Hoxie Neale Fairchild, *Religious Trends in English Poetry,* 6 vols. (New York: Columbia University Press, 1939–62), vol. 1, *Protestantism and the Cult of Sentiment, 1700–1740,* p. 130, respectively.

3. Cf. "I could never believe that Roughness and Obscurity added any thing to the true Grandeur of a Poem: nor will I ever affect Archaisms, Exoticisms, and a quaint Uncouthness of Speech, in order to become perfectly *Miltonian*" (preface to *Horae Lyricae,* pp. xx–xxi). It has been routine to see Watts "protesting with all of the power at his command against the sterility of Neo-classic poetry" (Arthur Paul Davis, *Isaac Watts: His Life and Works* (New York: Dryden Press, 1943), p. 162. An exception is John Hoyles, who seems to go to the opposite extreme in *The Waning of the Renaissance, 1640–1740: Studies in the Thought and Poetry of Henry More, John Norris, and Isaac Watts* (The Hague: Martinus Nijhoff, 1971).

4. For Watts's preface and the hymns we used the edition by Selma L. Bishop, *Hymns and Spiritual Songs* (London: Faith Press, 1962). The hymn numbers refer to book II unless otherwise indicated.

5. Watts commented further in his preface: "If the Verse appears so gentle and flowing as to incur the Censure of Feebleness, I may honestly affirm, that sometimes it cost me Labour to make it so: Some of the Beauties of Poesy are neglected, and some willfully defac'd: I have thrown out the Lines that were too sonorous, and have given an Allay to the Verse, lest a more exalted Turn of Thought or Language should darken or disturb the Devotion of the weakest Souls"(p. liv).

6. See further discussion of "Devotional Response," below. K.L. Parry noted the tension unavoidable in a Calvinist position influenced by eighteenth-century rationalism, in "Isaac Watts: Hymn-Writer and Divine," *Listener* 40 (December 2, 1948): 841–42. Hoyles considers Watts's solution to this conflict important in the intellectual history of the age *(Waning of the Renaissance,* p. 156).

7. An interesting seventy-year-old article in the *Edinburgh Review* suggested that the appeal of Roman Catholic ceremonial was transferred to Protestant hymns: "The Figure had been taken from the Crucifix, the Pietà by the roadway was shattered, the Stations effaced from the wall; but Wesley wrote with a painter's brush—'Who is this that comes from far, / Clad in garments dipped in blood?'" ("Hymnology, Classic and Romantic," *ER* 208 [July 1908]: 67). The idea better suits the hymns of Watts.

8. As an older man, Watts wrote extensively on the psychology of religious passions and their place in devotional life. The governance of "Affections by the sacred Dictates of Reason and Religion" promises to prevent bigotry and the madness of persecution. The aesthetic corollary of such discipline would be: "Bend the more lawful and useful Passions of *Love, Desire, Joy, Fear, Anger* and *Sorrow,* like young Trees, into a beautiful and regular Form, and prune off all their luxuriant Branches." Not surprisingly, sermons are to be shorn of emotional appeals, "a mere Explication of the Word of God, without inforcing these Things on the Conscience, by a pathetick Address to the Heart . . . , without seeking to awaken any of the devout Sensations of Hope and Fear, and Love and Joy, tho' the God of Nature hath ordained them to be the most effectual Allurements or Spurs to Duty in this present animal State." Citations refer, respectively, to Watts's preface to his *Discourses on the Love of God and the Use and Abuse of the Passions in Religion: With a devout Meditation suited to each Discourse. To which is prefixed, A plain and particular Account of the Natural Passions, with Rules for the Government of them* (London, 1729), pp. viii–ix; and to *The Doctrine of the Passions, Explain'd and Improv'd; or, A brief and comprehensive Scheme of the Natural Affections of Mankind, attempted in a plain and easy Method; with an Account of their Names, Nature, Appearances, Effects, and different Uses in human Life: to which are subjoin'd Moral and Divine Rules For the Regulation or Government of them* (1729; 3rd ed., corrected and enlarged, London: Hett, 1739). Contrast Charles Wesley's recollection of a successful sermon: "Now the power and blessing came. My mouth and their hearts were opened. The rocks were broken in pieces, and melted into tears on every side. I continued exhorting them, from seven till ten, to save themselves from this untoward generation. We could hardly part. I left the little society of twenty members confirmed and comforted." The passage is cited by Robert Newton Flew in *The Hymns of Charles Wesley: A Study of Their Structure* (London: Epworth Press, 1953), p. 38.

9. A second illustration is hymn CLXX, "God Incomprehensible and Sovereign."

10. Given the considerable treatment of hellfire in the hymns, Martha England's report is problematic: "Watts made no secret of how he searched the Bible for refutation of the belief in eternal punishment, could not find it, sadly reported what

he found, and said as little about it as conscience would allow" (Martha England and John Sparrow, *Hymns Unbidden: Donne, Herbert, Blake, Emily Dickinson, and the Hymnographers* [New York: New York Public Library,1966], p. 80).

11. Hoyles, so perceptive in his reading of Watts's theories, fails in his reading of hymns, as he tries to force them to conform to his thesis: "Classicism shunned the particular vision, sensory or imaginative; and there can be few poets so consistent in their avoidance of the visual than Watts" *(Waning of the Renaissance,* p. 236).

12. See discussion and bibliographic references provided in chapter 1, particularly the work of René Wellek, W. P. Friederich, and Marc Bertonasco.

13. Cf. Robert Stevenson: "At least he later had perspicuity enough to discard the language of physical rapture which pervades the Divine Love poems in his 1706 volume." "Dr. Watts' 'Flights of Fancy,'" *Harvard Theological Review* 42 (October 1949): 245.

14. "I think I may be bold to assert, that I never compos'd one Line of them with any other Design than what they are apply'd to here; and I have endeavour'd to secure them all from being perverted and debas'd to wanton Passions, by several Lines in them that can never be apply'd to a meaner Love"—preface to *Horae Lyricae* (1709), pp. xvi–xvii. Watts's later regrets are seen in his preface to *Devout Exercises of the Heart in Meditation and Soliloquy, Prayer and Praise,* by Elizabeth Rowe, "Reviewed and Published at her request by I. Watts D.D." (1737; 6th ed., 1754): "But if I may be permitted to speak the Sense of maturer Age, I can hardly think this the happiest Language in which Christians should generally discover their warm Sentiments of Religion, since the clearer and more spiritual Revelations of the New Testament" (pp. 10–11).

CHAPTER THREE

1. Citations from Charles S. Phillips, *Hymnody Past and Present* (New York: Macmillan, 1937), p. 171, and John Wesley, *Works,* vol. 14 (Grand Rapids, Mich.: Zondervan, 1872), p. 341. Fairchild has denied that Methodism had anything to do with worldly reason or learning *(Religious Trends in English Poetry,* 6 vols. [New York: Columbia University Press, 1939–62], vol. 2, *Religious Sentimentalism in the Age of Johnson, 1740–1780).* John Wesley's first hymn book, published in Georgia in 1737, was designed for use in Church of England congregations, although it was never officially adopted. Charles Wesley contributed nothing to this book. Cf. *John Wesley's First Hymn Book; a collection of Psalms and Hymns* (1737; facsimile ed., Charleston: Dalcho Historical Society, 1964). Martha England lists the contents of this volume in Martha England and John Sparrow, *Hymns Unbidden: Donne, Herbert, Blake, Emily Dickinson, and the Hymnographers* (New York: New York Public Library, 1966). Considerable evidence indicates that John and Charles were not always in agreement. See Thomas Walter Herbert, *John Wesley as Editor and Author* (Princeton: Princeton University Press, 1940).

2. Hymn 79, *Representative Verse of Charles Wesley,* ed. Frank Baker (London: Epworth Press, 1962). The quantity of Charles Wesley's hymns is awe inspiring and presents obvious problems to the student attempting to characterize them. In an oeuvre of 9,000 hymns, illustrations may be found of practically any devotional mood, theological attitude, or use of the hymn kind. Further, there is no authoritative canon of Wesley's work. The 1780 *Collection of Hymns for the Use of the People Called the Methodists* excludes many items and lacks important bibliographic indexes. The hymns of Wesley in modern use have been selected on principles, including liturgical use, unrelated to those of their composition. As a compromise between sweeping inclusion of all 9,000 and an arbitrary selection, we have chosen to cite only those hymns reproduced in

Baker's *Representative Verse,* trusting that such a representative selection would be most manageable and most objective. The usefulness of the textual variations cataloged by Baker is illustrated by the cuts made in hymn XVII.

3. The preacher played a key part both in the revival drama of field meetings and as an exemplary convert who knew firsthand the effects of personal salvation. Near the end of this chapter we will examine a special collection of hymns for the use of Methodist preachers as further evidence of the double dramatic achievement of Methodism.

4. John Wesley's approval of Watts's hymns is reflected in the 1737 collection, which contains thirty-five hymns by Watts in a total of seventy-five, the balance consisting either of translations of German Pietist hymns or of adaptations of seventeenth-century English devotional lyrics. Certainly the exclusion of Watts from the history of hymn writing, for example by the more enthusiastic historians of Methodist hymnody (such as Frederick Gill in *Charles Wesley: the First Methodist* [New York: Abingdon Press, 1964]), is unjustified.

5. Moravian hymns, with which Charles Wesley was familiar, provided one precedent. "Instead of being addressed to God, they were addressed to fellow-worshippers, and were *about* God" (Clifford W. Towlson, *Moravian and Methodist: Relationships and Influences in the Eighteenth Century* [London: Epworth Press, 1957], p. 31).

6. The longer poems of Richard Crashaw exhibit the same tendency to shift address. Wesley's multiple or illogically combined metaphors are sometimes very effective. In the following lines, for example, the wings of the dove send down light on our spiritual night rather than shading us, which would be their more normal function: "Expand Thy Wings, Prolific Dove, / Brood o'er our Nature's Night; / On our disorder'd Spirits move, / And let there now be Light" (XIII, 3). Martha England would disagree: "Wesley's poetry almost wrecks itself on his stubborn commitment to clarity. Denied the bolting-holes of obscurity, mixed metaphor, conceit, mysticism, and abstraction, he is hard put to it to render an honest report on his experience with a Reality that comprehends within itself all paradox, all symbol, all counter-symbol" (England and Sparrow, *Hymns Unbidden,* p. 100). Robert Newton Flew insisted that the Wesley hymns are practically expository: "This habit of orderly composition is due to his desire to teach Christian doctrine to ordinary people. Their counterpart in prose would be orderly sermons with the divisions clearly marked, as contrasted with sermons destitute of divisions" *(The Hymns of Charles Wesley: A Study of Their Structure* [London: Epworth Press, 1953], p. 18).

7. In terms of German hymn history, the use of blood and wounds follows the enthusiastic Moravian model of "lovely side hole" rather than the Pietist model.

8. England and Sparrow, *Hymns Unbidden,* p. 91.

9. J. Ernest Rattenbury, *The Evangelical Doctrines of Charles Wesley's Hymns* (London: Epworth Press, 1942), pp. 28–29.

10. Our answer to Rattenbury's questions is far from orthodox. Cf. Davis: "Watts is the classic, objective 'founder' of modern English hymnody; Wesley the poetic, highly emotional, romantic continuator of the tradition" (Arthur Paul Davis, *Isaac Watts: His Life and Works* [New York: Dryden Press, 1943], p. 215). Also, Frederick Luke Wiseman, who considered the hymns a *"Journal intime"* of Charles Wesley, conveying his mental states and emotional reactions (*Charles Wesley: Evangelist and Poet* [New York: Abingdon Press, 1932], p. 199).

11. J. Ernest Rattenbury, *The Eucharistic Hymns of John and Charles Wesley, to Which Is Appended Wesley's Preface Extracted from Brevint's Christian Sacrament and Sacrifice together with Hymns on the Lord's Supper* (London: Epworth Press, 1948), p. 69.

12. Jonathan Swift, no less experienced in Christian fellowship than Charles Wesley, wrote his *Verses on the Death of Dr. Swift* (1739) on the text from Rochefoucauld, which he translated: "In all distresses of our friends, / We first consult our private ends; /

While Nature, kindly bent to ease us, / Points out some circumstances to please us."
Sentiment and satire both aimed at correction.

13. *A Fine Picture of Enthusiasm* (London, 1744), cited by Umphrey Lee in *The Historical Backgrounds of Early Methodist Enthusiasm* (New York: Columbia University Press, 1931), p. 125.

CHAPTER FOUR

1. *The Works of the Reverend John Newton*, 6 vols. (New York: Williams & Whiting, 1810), vol. 1, *An Authentic Narrative of Some Remarkable and Interesting Particulars in the Life of * * * * * *, in Fourteen Letters.*
2. Bernard Martin, *John Newton: A Biography* (London: Heinemann, 1950).
3. Newton, *Works*, vol. 5, p. 570.
4. Preface to *Olney Hymns* in *The Works of the Reverend John Newton, Late rector of the United Parishes of St. Mary Woolnoth and St. Mary Woolchurch-Haw, Lombard Street, London* (Edinburgh: Thomas Nelson and Peter Brown, 1827), p. 523.
5. XXXVIII, stanza 7. Roman numerals refer to hymns of book I of *Olney Hymns* (*Works*, 1827) unless book II or III is indicated.
6. *Olney Hymns* (*Works*, 1827), p. 523
7. Hymn XII tells of the meeting between Joseph and the brothers who plotted against him. The first two stanzas describe the situation and the confusion of the brothers. Joseph then addresses them, and they express their amazement: "Though greatly distressed before, / When charg'd with purloining the cup, / They now were confounded much more, / Not one of them durst to look up. / 'Can Joseph, whom we would have slain, / Forgive us the evil we did? / And will he our households maintain? / O, this is a brother indeed!'"
8. Newton's radical position would seem to reflect the belief, held by some contemporary evangelicals, that Britain was the home of the lost tribes of Israel, an idea that gives the English a certain biblical status. On the other hand, the hymn portrayal of life at Olney in terms of cosmic relevance may be simply the work of Newton's dramatic imagination, the same imagination that awarded himself a heroic role in Christendom. (Cf. Newton, *Review of Ecclesiastical History* in *Works,* 1827, chapter 2, book II.)
9. Newton's providential view of history, deriving from the dynamic Calvinism of the Puritans, is by no means unique to him. Rather, it is commonplace among the Puritans, traceable through Tyndale to Deuteronomy. It is "prophetic" in the simplest sense of the word: "that understanding of history which accepts meaning only in terms of divine concern, divine purpose, divine participation." *(The Interpreter's Dictionary of the Bible,* vol. 3 [Nashville, Tenn.: Abingdon Press, 1962], p. 896.) Newton's interest in the American war was shared by John Wesley who, in *Hymns for the Nation* (1782), sees the rebellion as a divine instrument used to punish England for its rebellion against God.
10. Unlike Newton's greatest hymns, the historical-interpretive hymns have lost much of their appeal, the common fate of occasional verse. The series of hymns grouped under the heading "Providences" provides further illustration (II:LXIV–LXXI).

CHAPTER FIVE

1. Gilbert Thomas, *William Cowper and the Eighteenth Century* (London: Nicholson and Watson, 1935), p. 223. Almost all of the sixty-seven hymns that Cowper

provided for the Olney collection (1779) were written during 1771 and 1772, while he was living at Olney and helping Newton in parish work. Before the planned collection was completed, Cowper went insane, a circumstance suggesting that the hymns might reveal an increasingly disturbed mind and so be too subjective for communal use. Accordingly, much criticism has concerned itself with the subjectivity or conventionality of Cowper's hymns. The suitability for communal singing of statements as seemingly personal as the hymns has been debated. See Hoxie Neale Fairchild's *Religious Trends in English Poetry,* 6 vols. (New York: Columbia University Press, 1939–62), vol. 2, *Religious Sentimentalism in the Age of Johnson;* Wendell M. Keck's "Cowper's *Olney Hymns:* A Theological Study" (Ph.D. diss., Stanford University, 1941); Patricia Meyer Spacks's *The Poetry of Vision* (Cambridge, Mass.: Harvard University Press, 1967); Norman Nicholson's *William Cowper* (London: Longmans Green, 1951); and Lodwick Hartley's "The Worm and the Thorn: A Study of Cowper's *Olney Hymns,*" *Journal of Religion* 29 (1949): 220–29.

2. Cowper's hymns are taken from his *Life and Works,* ed. T.S. Grimshawe (New York: Robert Carter, 1849). Given the complex textual history of the *Olney Hymns* and the arbitrary nature of many editorial decisions, it was not deemed necessary to conform to the readings of the Oxford edition (*The Poems of William Cowper,* ed. John D. Baird and Charles Ryskamp, 1980), which came to the authors' attention after this book was set in type. Stanza numbers have been supplied as necessary.

3. While the butterfly is a common Christian symbol of the resurrection, the unlovely "winged worm" emphasizes the creature's fallen ignobility. One recalls George Eliot's admiration for hymn LI: "Do you remember Cowper's Hymn beginning 'I was a grovelling creature once.' It is lovely and rich as the pomegranate and the vine." *The George Eliot Letters,* ed. Gordon S. Haight, vol. 1 (New Haven: Yale University Press, 1954), p. 100. For a discussion of this imagery, see Maurice Quinlan, "Cowper's Imagery," *Journal of English and Germanic Philology* 47 (1948), and Hartley's "The Worm and the Thorn."

4. This hymn, which places Cowper squarely in the revival and dissenting hymn tradition, has provoked great furor among critics and hymnologists. To many it appears gruesome and distasteful, properly omitted from decent hymnbooks. Others find it intensely moving and powerful. The source of the power is variously ascribed. Norman Nicholson, for example, sees the strength of the hymn in the suggestion of "rituals even older than the Old Testament: of the dying god of the fertility cults and of primitive symbols that probe deeply into the subconscious mind" (*William Cowper,* p. 16). The hymn has given rise to a miracle literature of its own, vivid proof that the hymn has worked on the most hardened of sinners.

5. This understanding of the Crucifixion as exemplary suits the Wesleyan hymn model rather than that of Watts. The theology, traceable at least to Abelard, is Roman Catholic rather than Protestant and is not at all like that of Wesley. *The Works of Madame Guyon,* which Cowper translated into English, are a likely influence.

6. To some extent, Cowper's difficulty with apparent evil in creation, comparable to Voltaire's troubles, simply marks the obsolescence of natural religion with its confidence in the rightness of Creation by an artificer God. Within the Olney collection, Cowper's fears balance Newton's providential view of history in the same manner that Job and Ecclesiastes balance the providential view maintained in much of the Hebrew Bible. At issue is the impracticability of congregational hymns that raise more questions than they answer or that express fear, then attempt consolation, and fail.

7. Isaiah 10 and Hebrews 12 provide scriptural precedents for the disciplinary image. The difference here is our fear of being cast away, the powerful craving for

punishment and abasement, and the suggestion that we are saved by our own suffering. (Cf. Cowper's exemplary Crucifixion hymns, particularly XXVIII and XLIV.)

CHAPTER SIX

1. Frederick Gill, *The Romantic Movement and Methodism: A Study of English Romanticism and the Evangelical Revival* (London: Epworth Press, 1937).

2. Thomas B. Shepherd, *Methodism and the Literature of the Eighteenth Century* (London: Epworth Press, 1940); Jacob Bronowski, *William Blake and the Age of Revolution* (New York: Harper and Row, 1965); Martha England and John Sparrow, *Hymns Unbidden: Donne, Herbert, Blake, Emily Dickinson, and the Hymnographers* (New York: New York Public Library, 1966). The last book contains a full discussion of the relationship between the ideas of Blake and those of Charles Wesley.

3. Harold Bloom, "Blake's *Jerusalem:* The Bard of Sensibility and the Form of Prophecy," *Eighteenth-Century Studies* 4 (1970): 6–20, p. 10.

4. This quotation concerns Shelley's early prose *Address to the Irish People,* which is less successful than the later "Song" but shares with it the extreme language and the heavy irony reminiscent of the false doctrine hymns.

5. *The Poetical Works of Shelley,* ed. Newell F. Ford (Boston: Houghton Mifflin, 1975), pp. 374–75. Shelley was of course exposed to organized religion and to the Bible, by whose language he was clearly influenced. In his dealings with workmen, especially in North Wales, he may also have been directly exposed to the evangelical hymn.

6. *The Poetry and Prose of William Blake,* ed. David V. Erdman, commentary by Harold Bloom (Garden City, New York: Doubleday, 1965), pp. 94–95.

7. Ibid., p. 170.

8. Louis Benson, *The English Hymn: Its Development and Use in Worship* (New York: Hodder and Stoughton, 1915), p. 340.

9. See Byron's *Hebrew Melodies* and renderings of the psalms; Wordsworth's "Labourer's noonday Hymn"; and Thomas Moore's "Sacred Song."

10. *Hymns, written and adapted to the weekly church service of the year* (London: John Murray, 1827), p. 25. Compare "Hark the Herald Angels Sing." The stirring tunes to which these hymns were sung had an important part in their popularity. The history of the hymn tunes—which we have been unable to provide—would doubtless contribute to the explanation of the change in the hymn after Cowper as it would supplement and enhance our understanding of the hymns treated in these chapters.

11. Ibid., p. 92.

12. Ibid., p. 139.

Index